AIR FRYER COOKBOOK

2023

MEAT EDITION

*The Best 100+ Quick And Easy Recipes
For Juicy And Delicious Meat That You Can Cook
Every Day With Your Family.*

PETER STEAK

Disclaimer Notice:

Please note the information contained within this document is for educational and entertainment purposes only. All effort has been executed to present accurate, up to date, and reliable, complete information. No warranties of any kind are declared or implied. Readers acknowledge that the author is not engaging in the rendering of legal, financial, medical or professional advice. The content within this book has been derived from various sources. Please consult a licensed professional before attempting any techniques outlined in this book.

By reading this document, the reader agrees that under no circumstances is the author responsible for any losses, direct or indirect, which are incurred as a result of the use of information contained within this document, including, but not limited to, errors, omissions, or inaccuracies.

Table of Contents

INTRODUCTION

Nothing is quite as satisfying as the sound of a crisp, savory fry coming out of the skillet. Some people will argue that french fries are simply not complete without ketchup, while others prefer to drench their crispy fried potatoes in honey or homemade mayonnaise. In recent years, an alternative cooking technique has emerged in kitchens all across the world. Gone are the days when frying food required constant attention and a deep fryer full of sizzling oil. Air frying, a combination of existing technology and good old-fashioned culinary know-how, has taken chefs and cooks by storm.

Air fryers use an air circulation technology to trap the heat produced by a heating element. The heat is then distributed around the food being cooked, cooking it from all sides at once. This means no more standing around for hours, waiting for a pot of oil to get hot enough to cook your favorite dishes!

Benefits of the Air Fryer

1. Healthy Cooking

So, how would anything be healthy if it's fried? It's easy! These machines may be used without using any oil whatsoever or with only a squirt of oil if you like. You can fry frozen fries, onion rings, wings, and more without adding any additional oil yet still get very crispy results. The fries from the air fryer are crispier, but it's not as dry as those from the oven, and using this to prepare breaded zucchini wedges is far more impressive!

2. Efficient Meals

They cook food quickly because they are small than that of an oven and disperse the air with fans. Preheating an oven will take up to 20-30 minutes, while these fryers get up to temperature in minutes. You'll actually enjoy this time-saver whether you need to prepare snacks or meals quickly.

3. Flexibility

This is perhaps the main aspect of an air fryer. There's so much you can do about it! Yes, as opposed to an oven, it fries very well. However, it may also bake (including cakes), broil, roast, barbecue, and stir fry! If you want to eat chicken & snow peas for brunch? For one of these, it's simple to create. You will use them to prepare both fresh & frozen Ingredients, as well as to reheat leftovers. Meats, seafood, casseroles, wraps, and a variety of vegetables have all been prepared in there. A grill rack, grill tray, or raised cooking rack are used in some fryers. Since the baskets can be divided, you can prepare several recipes at the same time. It's amazing that a single system may cook this many different foods in so many varying ways.

4. Space-Saving Device

This advantage can be useful whether you have a limited kitchen or reside in a dorm room or communal accommodation. The majority of these machines are equivalent to a coffee maker. They don't take up a lot of space on the counter and are normally simple to store or transfer. They can substitute other devices like a toaster, and also some people use them in cooking facilities or RVs where a real oven isn't available. They're even very useful in a workplace break space!

5. Usability

Most fryers are simple to operate; simply set the temperature and cooking time, add the food, then shake the fryer a few times during cooking. There's no reason to mess or swirl as you might on a stovetop. The baskets allow shaking the food easy and fast, and the device doesn't lose much heat when it's opened. So, if you want to glimpse when preparing, go ahead! You won't be speeding it down as you would in an oven if you do this.

6. Cleaning Ease

Clean-up is one aspect of cooking that many of us dislike. You just need to clean an air fryer's basket and plate, and many of those are dishwasher safe. Food does not adhere to non-stick coated areas of the pan but instead slips straight down onto the plate. It just takes a couple of minutes to clean up after each use. This encourages you to prepare more at home, so you don't have to worry about cleaning up!

7. Efficient Energy Usage

Such fryers are more effective than utilizing an oven and would not overheat your home. You would be surprised by how powerful these machines are whether you are striving to hold your house comfortable throughout the summer or are concerned about your electric bill.

Healthful Benefits

When used correctly, air fryers have a slew of health benefits:

1. Air fryers will help you lose weight.

Fried food use is directly linked to an increased risk of obesity. This is due to the high fat and calorie content of deep-fried foods. Weight reduction may be aided by switching from deep-fried to air-fried foods and lowering the daily consumption of unhealthy oils.

2. Air fryers have the potential to be safer than deep fryers.

Deep-frying foods necessitate the use of a huge container filled with hot oil. This may be dangerous. Though air fryers also get heated, there is no danger of dropping, splashing or handling hot oil by mistake. To ensure protection, people can use frying appliances carefully and follow directions.

3. The chance of poisonous acrylamide forming is reduced by using an air fryer.

Frying food in oil may result in the formation of harmful compounds like acrylamide. Through high-heat cooking processes, such as deep-frying, this compounds exists in some foods. Acrylamide has been linked to the growth of cancers such as endometrial, ovarian, pancreatic, breast, as well as esophageal cancer, as per the International Agency for Research on Cancer. People may reduce the chance of acrylamide contamination in their food by converting to air frying.

4. Reducing the intake of deep-fried foods lowers the risk of illness.

Cooking with oil and eating traditional fried foods on a daily basis has been linked to a variety of health problems. Deep frying may be replaced with other cooking techniques to reduce the chance of these problems.

The 10 Rules of Perfect Frying

1. Even though they produce the same result, the fryer uses less oil than the frying pan. As a result, the review shows that the amount of oil used should be well measured.

2. Use a small amount of oil to keep the food from boiling.

3. Always make sure the fryer is oil-free at all times.

4. When the appliance starts to exhibit signs of inadequate cleanliness, such as a foul smell, white smoke, or the basket drawer failing to close, it is time for a thorough cleaning.

5. Since certain foods must be fried at high temperature, search for the best fryer on such occasion, mostly with nothing less than 200 degrees.

6. Choose your fryer based on the size of your household (the size of the basket), ease of use, and several features.

7. Some versions have a special "frying" mode for frying.

8. Since some fryers retain heat better than others, always factor in a slight difference in cooking time compared to the recipes in this book.

9. Some fryers have specific functions for each type of food; familiarize yourself with the one in your possession.

10. If the fryer is of high quality, the manufacturer can sell some handy separate attachment for even better use, and purchasing them may be a good idea.

Air Fryer Troubleshooting

White Smoke

White smoke may surface from your air fryer for a variety of reasons. If you are preparing food that is high in fat, the food may produce excess oil, which lingers in the air fryer. You may need to check in during the cooking process and soak up any excess oil with a paper towel. Once the oil is cleaned up, resume cooking. White smoke will not harm the air fryer. Smoke may also surface if the air fryer is not properly cleaned in between each use. Check to ensure there isn't any oil left in the bottom of the air fryer from previous use.

Black Smoke

Black smoke should not surface from your air fryer. If you notice black smoke, turn off and unplug the machine immediately, and consult with the manufacturer.

Not Crisping

If you notice that your food is not browning or becoming crisp, you may not have added enough oil. Try adding a little additional oil. Make sure you have not overcrowded the air fryer basket and that you have flipped food repeatedly throughout the cooking process.

RECIPES

1. Herbed Roast Chicken

Preparation Time: 35 minutes

Cooking Time: 1 hr. 30 minutes

Servings: 8

Ingredients: :

- 1 whole chicken
- 2 tbsp olive oil
- 1 tsp garlic powder
- 1 tsp paprika
- ½ tsp oregano
- 1 tablespoon Salt and black pepper to taste
- 1 lemon, cut into quarters
- 5 garlic cloves

Directions: :

1. In a bowl, combine olive oil, garlic powder, paprika, oregano, salt, and pepper, and mix well to make a paste. Rub the chicken with the paste and stuff lemon and garlic cloves into the cavity.

2. Place the chicken in the air fryer, breast side down, and tuck the legs and wings tips under. Bake for 45 minutes at 360 F. Flip the chicken to breast side up and cook for another 15-20 minutes. Let rest for 5-6 minutes, then carve, and serve.

Nutrition: Calories: 280, Fat: 5.7g, Fiber: 12.1g, Carbs: 40.7g, Protein: 12.9g

2.   Grilled Chicken and Radish Mix Recipe

Preparation Time: 20 minutes

Cooking Time: 40 Minutes

Servings: 4

Ingredients: :

- bone-in chicken things; -4
- 1 tablespoon Salt and black pepper to the taste
- Olive oil 1 tbsp.
- carrots; cut into thin sticks 3
- Chopped chives; -2 tbsp.
- chicken stock-128 g
- sugar128 g
- radishes; halved-6

Directions: :

1. Start by Heating a container that accommodates your air fryer over medium warmth, include stock, carrots, sugar, and radishes; mix delicately,
2. Reduce warmth to medium, spread pot somewhat and permit to stew for 20 minutes.
3. Coat the chicken with olive oil, season with salt and pepper, put in your air fryer and cook at 350 °F, for 4 minutes.
4. Introduce the chicken to radish blend and hurl appropriately
5. Introduce everything in your air fryer, cook for 4 minutes more,
6. Share among plates and serve.

Nutrition:

Calories: 314, Fat: 15.4g, Fiber: 10.1g, Carbs: 28.7g, Protein: 22.4g

3.   Quail in White Wine Sauce

Preparation Time: 12 hrs.

Cooking Time: 90 minutes

Servings: 4

Ingredients: :

- 4 large quail
- 1 bottle of dry white wine
- 1 tsp of sweet paprika
- 1 tsp of hot paprika
- ½ package fresh sage, chopped or 2 tbsp dehydrated sage
- 1 head minced garlic
- ¼ tsp of virgin olive oil
- 1.7 oz. of butter
- 1 tablespoon Salt to taste
- 4 rosemary sprigs

Directions: :

1. The recipe is very easy; it should only be prepared well in advance.
2. Wash the quail well. Boil salted water in a skillet enough to cover the quail.
3. When the water boils, place the quail in the pan and cover for 5 minutes.
4. Drain and let cool. Put a little minced garlic inside each quail. Place the quail in a large bowl and top with white wine. Add sweet bell pepper, hot pepper, olive oil, and sage. Marinate in the seasoning in the refrigerator for at least 12 hours. Remove the quail from the seasoning and place it in a pan with butter.
5. Take to the preheated air fryer to about 2000F and bake for 90 minutes.
6. Open the oven every 15 minutes and turn the quails and sprinkle with the marinade.

Nutrition: Calories: 319, Fat: 19g, Fiber: 16.1g, Carbs: 78g, Protein: 21.1g

4. Caribbean Chicken Thighs

Preparation Time: 30 minutes

Cooking Time: 10 minutes

Servings: 8

Ingredients: :

- Chicken thigh fillets: 1kg. boneless and skinless
- 1 tablespoon Ground black pepper
- Ground coriander seed: 1 tablespoon
- 1 tablespoon Salt
- Ground cinnamon: 1 tablespoon
- Cayenne pepper: 1 tablespoon
- Ground ginger: 1 ½ teaspoons
- Ground nutmeg: 1 ½ teaspoons
- Coconut oil: 3 tablespoons

Directions: :

1. Take chicken off the packaging and pat dry. To soak up any residual liquid, place on a large baking sheet covered with paper towels. Chicken is salted and peppered on both sides. Let the chicken sit for 30 minutes, so when you go into the air fryer, it isn't that cold.
2. Combine cilantro, cinnamon, cayenne, ginger, and nutmeg in a small bowl. Coat the spice mixture on each piece of chicken and brush both sides with coconut oil.
3. Place four pieces of chicken in your air fryer basket (they shouldn't overlap). Air fry for 10 minutes at 390 degrees F. Remove the chicken from the basket and place it in a safe stove dish, tightly covered with foil.
4. Keep the chicken in the oven to keep it warm until the remaining chicken is done — repeat the instructions for air frying with the rest of the chicken.

Nutrition: Calories: 276, Fat: 6.4g, Fiber: 12.1g, Carbs: 56.5g, Protein: 13.1g

5.   Chicken Coconut Meatballs

Preparation Time: 10 minutes

Cooking Time: 10 minutes

Servings: 4

Ingredients: :

- 453 g ground chicken
- 1 ½ tsp sriracha
- 1/2 tbsp soy sauce
- 1/2 tbsp hoisin sauce
- 32 g shredded coconut
- 1 tsp sesame oil
- 64 g fresh cilantro, chopped
- 2 green onions, chopped
- 1 tablespoon Pepper
- 1 tablespoon Salt

Directions: :

1. Spray air fryer basket with cooking spray.
2. Add all Ingredients into the large bowl and mix until well combined.
3. Make small balls from meat mixture and place into the air fryer basket.
4. Cook at 350 F for 10 minutes. Turn halfway through.
5. Serve and enjoy.

Nutrition: Calories: 180, Fat: 1.3g, Fiber: 2.4g, Carbs: 11.5g, Protein: 10.1g

6.   Chicken Pasta Salad

Preparation Time: 20 minutes

Cooking Time: 25-30 minutes

Servings: 4

Ingredients: :

- 3 chicken breasts - 1 tablespoon Paprika
- 1 medium bag frozen vegetables of choice
- 128 g rigatoni or pasta of choice; cooked
- 1 tablespoon Garlic and herb seasoning
- Italian dressing - 1 tablespoon Black pepper
- 1 tablespoon Ground parsley
- 1 tablespoon Oil spray

Directions: :

1. Wash the chicken breasts and season with paprika, garlic and herb seasoning and a tbsp. of the Italian dressing. Top a little with black pepper and ground parsley. Mist the air fryer with oil, then add the marinated chicken breasts. Spray oil over the chicken as well. Cook at 360°F for 15 minutes

2. Halfway through, flip the chicken breasts and season with pepper and parsley. Spray over with oil and allow to cook all the way

3. While the chicken is cooking, empty a bag of frozen vegetables into a bowl and season with the garlic and herb dressing and some Italian dressing. Mix well. Spray another air fryer and add in the vegetables. Cook for 12 minutes at 380°F.

4. Dice the cooked chicken while waiting for the vegetables to cook. Season the cooked with some garlic and herb seasoning, along with some parsley and Italian dressing

5. Mix well, tasting to your preference. Add the diced chicken to the mix, mixing well. Once the vegetables have finished cooking, add to the chicken and pasta mixture and incorporate thoroughly. Serve

Nutrition: Calories: 265, Fat: 8.5g, Fiber: 14.1g, Carbs: 45.9g, Protein: 15.6 g

7.   Chicken Marinara

Preparation Time: 20 minutes

Cooking Time: 15 minutes

Servings: 2

Ingredients: :

- ½ C. keto marinara - 6 tbsp. mozzarella cheese
- 1 tbsp. melted ghee - 1kg chicken breasts
- 2 tbsp. grated parmesan cheese
- 6 tbsp. gluten-free seasoned breadcrumbs

Directions: :

1. Ensure air fryer is preheated to 360 degrees. Spray the basket with olive oil.
2. Mix parmesan cheese and breadcrumbs together. Melt ghee. Brush melted ghee onto the chicken and dip into breadcrumb mixture. Place coated chicken in the air fryer and top with olive oil. Cook 2 breasts for 6 minutes and top each breast with a tablespoon of sauce and 1 ½ tablespoons of mozzarella cheese. Cook another 3 minutes to melt cheese. Keep cooked pieces warm as you repeat the process with remaining breasts.

Nutrition: Calories: 265, Fat: 8.5g, Fiber: 11.1g, Carbs: 39.6g, Protein: 15.6 g

8. Chicken Burrito

Preparation Time: 20 minutes

Cooking Time: 10 minutes

Servings: 4

Ingredients: :

- 4 chicken breast slices; cooked and shredded
- 2 tortillas
- 1 avocado; peeled, pitted and sliced
- 1 green bell pepper; sliced
- 2 eggs; whisked
- 2 tbsp. mild salsa
- 2 tbsp. cheddar cheese; grated
- 1 tablespoon Salt and black pepper to taste

Directions: :

1. In a bowl, whisk the eggs with the salt and pepper and pour them into a pan that fits your air fryer. Put the pan in the air fryer's basket, cook for 5 minutes at 400°F and transfer the mix to a plate

2. Place the tortillas on a working surface and between them divide the eggs, chicken, bell peppers, avocado and the cheese; roll the burritos

3. Line your air fryer with tin foil, add the burritos and cook them at 300°F for 3-4 minutes. Serve for breakfast-or lunch, or dinner!

Nutrition: Calories: 287, Fat: 4.6g, Fiber: 8.1g, Carbs: 34.7g, Protein: 9.1g

9.   Parmesan Garlic Wings

Preparation Time: 20 minutes

Cooking Time: 30 minutes

Servings: 4

Ingredients: :

- Raw chicken wings – 1kg
- Salt – 1 tsp. - Garlic powder – ½ tsp.
- Baking powder – 1 tbsp.
- Unsalted butter – 4 tbsps. melted
- Grated Parmesan cheese – 96 g
- Dried parsley – ¼ tsp.

Directions: :

1. Place chicken wings, salt, ½ tsp. garlic powder, and baking powder in a bowl. Coat and place wings into the air fryer basket. Cook at 400F for 25 minutes. Toss the basket two or 3 times during the cooking time. Combine butter, parmesan, and parsley in a bowl. Remove wings from the air fryer and place into a bowl. Pour the butter mixture over the wings and toss to coat. Serve warm

Nutrition: Calories: 281, Fat: 5.7g, Fiber: 9.4g, Carbs: 22.6g, Protein: 12.1g

10.   Creamy Coconut Chicken

Preparation Time: 20 minutes

Cooking Time: 30 minutes

Servings: 4

Ingredients: :

- Big chicken legs – 4 - Turmeric powder – 5 tsps.
- Ginger – 2 tbsps. grated
- Salt and black pepper to taste
- Coconut cream – 4 tbsps.

Directions: :

1. In a bowl, mix salt, pepper, ginger, turmeric, and cream.
2. Whisk.
3. Add chicken pieces, coat and marinate for 2 hours.
4. Transfer chicken to the preheated air fryer and cook at 370F for 25 minutes.
5. Serve.

Nutrition: Calories: 221 Fat: 1.9g, Fiber: 1.91g Carbs: 14.5g Protein: 12.4g

11. Chinese Duck Legs

Preparation Time: 30 minutes

Cooking Time: 35 minutes

Servings: 2

Ingredients: :

- Duck legs – 2
- Dried chilies – 2, chopped
- Olive oil – 1 tbsp.
- Star anise – 2
- Spring onions – 1 bunch, chopped
- Ginger – 4 slices
- Oyster sauce – 1 tbsp.
- Soy sauce – 1 tbsp.
- Sesame oil – 1 tsp.
- Water – 500ml
- Rice wine – 1 tbsp.

Directions: :

1. Heat oil in a pan. Add water, soy sauce, oyster sauce, ginger, rice wine, sesame oil, star anise, and chili. Stir and cook for 6 minutes.
2. Add spring onions and duck legs, toss to coat and transfer to a pan.
3. Place the pan in the air fryer and cook at 370F for 30 minutes. Serve.

Nutrition: Calories: 243, Fat: 2.7g, Fiber: 8.1g, Carbs: 16.7g, Protein: 11.1g

12. Stuffed Pork Chops

Preparation Time: 30 minutes

Cooking Time: 25-30 minutes

Servings: 8

Ingredients: :

- 8 pork chops-2kg
- ¼ tsp pepper
- 512 g stuffing mix
- ½ tsp salt
- 2 tbsp olive oil
- 4 garlic cloves, minced
- 2 tbsp sage leaves

Directions: :

1. Preheat your Air Fryer to 350 F.
2. Cut a hole in pork chops and fill chops with stuffing mix.
3. In a bowl, mix sage leaves, garlic cloves, oil, salt and pepper.
4. Cover chops with marinade and let marinate for 10 minutes.
5. Place the chops in your Air Fryer's cooking basket and cook for 25 minutes.
6. Serve and enjoy!

Nutrition: Calories: 315, Fat: 11.9g, Fiber: 4.7g, Carbs: 17g, Protein: 15.1g

13. Pork Sausage Ratatouille

Preparation Time: 40 minutes

Cooking Time: 50 minutes

Servings: 6

Ingredients: :

- 4 pork sausages
- For Ratatouille
- 1 pepper, chopped - 2 zucchinis, chopped
- 1 eggplant, chopped
- 1 medium red onion, chopped
- 1 tbsp olive oil - 1-ounce butterbean, drained
- 5 tomatoes, chopped
- 2 sprigs fresh thyme
- 1 tbsp balsamic vinegar
- 2 garlic cloves, minced
- 1 red chili, chopped

Directions: :

1. Preheat your Air Fryer to 392 F. Mix pepper, eggplant, oil, onion, zucchinis, and add to the cooking basket. Roast for 20 minutes. Set aside to cool. Reduce Air Fryer temperature to 356 F. In a saucepan, mix prepared vegetables and the remaining ratatouille Ingredients, and bring to a boil over medium heat.
2. Let the mixture simmer for 10 minutes; season with salt and pepper. Add sausages to your Air Fryer's basket and cook for 10-15 minutes. Serve the sausages with ratatouille.

Nutrition: Calories: 341 Fat: 10.5g, Fiber: 12g Carbs: 11.7g Protein: 14.1g

14.   Sticky Pork Ribs

Preparation Time: 30 minutes

Cooking Time: 45 minutes

Servings: 6

Ingredients: :

- 1kg pork ribs - 2 tbsp char siew sauce
- 2 tbsp minced ginger
- 2 tbsp hoisin sauce
- 2 tbsp sesame oil - 1 tbsp honey
- 4 garlic cloves, minced - 1 tbsp soy sauce

Directions: :

1. Whisk together all marinade Ingredients in a small bowl; coat the ribs well with the mixture. Place in a container with a lid, and refrigerate for 4 hours. Preheat the air fryer to 330 F.

2. Place the ribs in the basket but do not throw away the liquid from the container; cook for 40 minutes. Stir in the liquid, increase the temperature to 350 F, and cook 10 more minutes.

Nutrition: Calories: 290 Fat: 9.7g, Fiber: 10.9g Carbs: 15.6g Protein: 19.5g

15.   Pork Sausage with Mashed Cauliflower

Preparation Time: 20 minutes

Cooking Time: 30 minutes

Servings: 6

Ingredients: :

- 453 g cauliflower, chopped
- 1/2 teaspoon tarragon
- 96 g Colby cheese
- 1/2 teaspoon ground black pepper
- 1/2 onion, peeled and sliced
- 1 teaspoon cumin powder
- 1/2 teaspoon sea salt
- 3 beaten eggs
- 6 pork sausages, chopped

Directions: :

1. Boil the cauliflower until tender. Then, purée the cauliflower in your blender. Transfer to a mixing dish along with the other Ingredients.
2. Divide the prepared mixture among six lightly greased ramekins; now, place ramekins in your air fryer.
3. Bake in the preheated Air Fryer for 27 minutes at 365 degrees F. Eat warm.

Nutrition: Calories: 320, Fat: 10.5g, Fiber: 9.5g, Carbs: 11.9g, Protein: 16.8 g

16.   Spicy Pork Meatballs

Preparation Time: 30 minutes

Cooking Time: 15 minutes

Servings: 4

Ingredients: :

- 453 g ground pork
- 128 g scallions, finely chopped
- 2 cloves garlic, finely minced
- 1 ½ tablespoons Worcester sauce
- 1 tablespoon oyster sauce
- 1 teaspoon turmeric powder
- 1/2 teaspoon freshly grated ginger root
- 1 small sliced red chili, for garnish

Directions: :

1. Mix all of the above Ingredients, apart from the red chili. Knead with your hands to ensure an even mixture.

2. Roll into equal balls and transfer them to the Air Fryer cooking basket. Set the timer for 15 minutes and push the power button. Air-fry at 350 degrees F. Sprinkle with sliced red chili; serve immediately with your favorite sauce for dipping. Enjoy!

Nutrition: Calories: 54 Fat: 6.7g, Fiber: 9.1g Carbs:11.5g Protein: 12.1g

17.   Hoisin Pork Loin

Preparation Time: 20 minutes

Cooking Time: 5-10 minutes

Servings: 4

Ingredients: :

- 2 tablespoons dry white wine
- 96 g hoisin sauce
- 2 teaspoons smoked cayenne pepper
- 3 garlic cloves, pressed
- 1/2-kg pork loin steak, cut into strips
- 3 teaspoons fresh lime juice
- 1 tablespoon Salt and ground black pepper, to taste

Directions: :

1. Start by preheating your Air Fryer to 395 degrees F.
2. Toss the pork with other Ingredients; let it marinate at least 20 minutes in a fridge.
3. Then, air-fry the pork strips for 5 minutes. Bon appétit!

Nutrition: Calories: 287, Fat: 5.6g, Fiber: 11.1g, Carbs: 14.5g, Protein: 18.5 g

18.   Pork Kebabs

Preparation Time: 35 minutes

Cooking Time: 18-20 minutes

Servings: 6

Ingredients: :

- 2 tablespoons tomato puree
- 1/2 fresh serrano, minced
- 1/3 teaspoon paprika
- 453 g pork, ground
- 64 g green onions, finely chopped
- 3 cloves garlic, peeled and finely minced
- 1 teaspoon ground black pepper, or more to taste
- 1 teaspoon salt, or more to taste

Directions: :

1. Thoroughly combine all Ingredients in a mixing dish. Then, form your mixture into sausage shapes.

2. Cook for 18 minutes at 355 degrees F. Mound salad on a serving platter, top with air-fried kebabs and serve warm. Bon appétit!

Nutrition: Calories: 267, Fat: 10.7g, Fiber: 15.4g, Carbs: 9.5g, Protein: 14.5 g

19. Bacon Wrapped Hotdogs

Preparation Time: 20 minutes

Cooking Time: 10-12 minutes

Servings: 5

Ingredients: :

- 10 thin slices of bacon
- 5 pork hot dogs, halved
- 1 teaspoon cayenne pepper
- Sauce:
- 32 g mayo
- 4 tablespoons ketchup, low-carb
- 1 teaspoon rice vinegar
- 1 teaspoon chili powder

Directions: :

1. Lay the slices of bacon on your working surface. Place a hot dog on one end of each slice; sprinkle with cayenne pepper and roll them over.
2. Cook in the preheated Air Fryer at 390 degrees F for 10 to 12 minutes.
3. Whisk all Ingredients for the sauce in a mixing bowl and store in your refrigerator, covered, until ready to serve.
4. Serve bacon-wrapped hot dogs with the sauce on the side. Enjoy!

Nutrition: Calories: 210, Fat: 5g, Fiber: 5.1g, Carbs: 10.5g, Protein: 11g

20. Cheesy Pork Casserole

Preparation Time: 30 minutes

Cooking Time: 16-20 minutes

Servings: 6

Ingredients: :

- 453 glean ground pork
- 1/2-kg ground beef
- 32 g tomato puree
- 1 tablespoon Sea salt and ground black pepper, to taste
- 1 teaspoon smoked paprika
- 1/2 teaspoon dried oregano
- 1 teaspoon dried basil
- 1 teaspoon dried rosemary
- 2 eggs
- 128 g Cottage cheese, crumbled, at room temperature
- 64 g Cotija cheese, shredded

Directions: :

1. Lightly grease a casserole dish with a nonstick cooking oil. Add the ground meat to the bottom of your casserole dish.
2. Add the tomato puree. Sprinkle with salt, black pepper, paprika, oregano, basil, and rosemary.
3. In a mixing bowl, whisk the egg with cheese. Place on top of the ground meat mixture. Place a piece of foil on top.
4. Bake in the preheated Air Fryer at 350 degrees F for 10 minutes; remove the foil and cook an additional 6 minutes. Bon appétit!

Nutrition: Calories: 298, Fat: 11.6g, Fiber: 10.5g, Carbs: 25.6g, Protein: 15.6g

21. Sherry-Braised Ribs

Preparation Time: 15 minutes

Cooking Time: 25-30 minutes

Servings: 4

Ingredients: :

- 1 rack ribs, cut in half to fit the Air Fryer
- 32 g sherry wine
- 2 tablespoons coconut amino
- 1 tablespoon Dijon mustard
- 1 tablespoon Sea salt and ground black pepper, to taste
- 128 g grape tomatoes
- 1 teaspoon dried rosemary

Directions: :

1. Toss the pork ribs with sherry wine, coconut aminos, mustard, salt, and black pepper.
2. Add the ribs to the lightly greased cooking basket. Cook in the preheated Air Fryer at 370 degrees F for 25 minutes.
3. Turn the ribs over, add the tomatoes and rosemary; cook an additional 5 minutes. Serve immediately.

Nutrition: Calories: 385 Fat: 11.6g, Fiber: 12.7g Carbs: 18.4g Protein: 22g

22. Air-fried Pork with Sweet and Sour Glaze

Preparation Time: 20 minutes

Cooking Time: 30 minutes

Servings: 6

Ingredients: :

- 32 g rice wine vinegar
- ¼ teaspoon Chinese five spice powder
- 128 g potato starch
- 1 green onion, chopped
- 2 large eggs, beaten
- 2 kg pork chops cut into chunks
- 2 tablespoons cornstarch + 3 tablespoons water
- 5 tablespoons brown Sugar
- 1 tablespoon Salt and pepper to taste

Directions: :

1. Preheat the air fryer oven to 390°f.
2. Season pork chops with salt and pepper to taste.
3. Dip the pork chops in egg. Set aside.
4. In a bowl, combine the potato starch and Chinese five spice powder.
5. Dredge the pork chops in the flour mixture.
6. Place in the double layer rack and cook for 30 minutes.
7. Meanwhile, place the vinegar and brown Sugar in a saucepan. Season with salt and pepper to taste. Stir in the cornstarch slurry and allow to simmer until thick.
8. Serve the pork chops with the sauce and garnish with green onions.

Nutrition: , Calories: 410 Fat: 15.9g, Fiber: 15.4g Carbs: 31.8g, Protein: 25g

23.   Lamb Kebabs

Preparation Time: 20 minutes

Cooking Time: 25-30 minutes

Servings: 6

Ingredients: :

- 453 g of lamb
- 3- onions chopped
- 5- green chilies-roughly chopped
- 1 ½- tbsp. ginger paste
- 1 ½- tsp garlic paste
- 1 ½- tsp salt
- 3 tsp lemon juice
- 2 tsp garam masala
- 4 tbsp. chopped coriander
- 3 tbsp. cream
- 4 tbsp. fresh mint chopped
- 3 tbsp. chopped capsicum
- 3 eggs
- 2 ½- tbsp. white sesame seeds

Directions: :

1. Mix the lamb with the ground ginger and cut green chilies.
2. Kg this blend until it turns into a thick paste. Add water if required.
3. Add the onions, mint, breadcrumbs and spices.
4. Blend this well until you get a soft mixture.
5. Form round kebabs with the dough.
6. Pour a small amount of milk onto each kebab to wet it.
7. Roll the kebab in the dry breadcrumbs.
8. Preheat the Air Fryer for 5 minutes at 300 F and cook for 30 minutes.
9. Recommended sides for this dish are mint chutney, tomato ketchup or yogurt chutney.

Nutrition: Calories: 188, Fat: 4.5g, Fiber: 9.1g, Carbs: 24.5g, Protein: 10.9g

24. Spiced Beef Fajitas

Preparation Time: 30 minutes

Cooking Time: 10 minutes

Servings: 8

Ingredients: :

- 453 g beef sirloin steak, cut into strips
- 2 garlic cloves, minced
- 1 tbsp paprika
- 1 red bell pepper, sliced
- 1 orange bell pepper, sliced
- 2 shallots, sliced
- 2 tbsp cajun seasoning
- 2 tbsp olive oil
- 8 tortilla wraps
- 64 g cheddar cheese, shredded
- 1 tablespoon Salt and black pepper to taste

Directions: :

1. Preheat the air fryer to 360 F.
2. In a bowl, combine the beef, shallots, bell peppers, and garlic. Season with Cajun seasoning, paprika, salt, and black pepper; toss to combine. Transfer the mixture to a greased baking dish and place in the air fryer basket. Bake for 10 minutes, shaking once or twice throughout cooking. Serve on tortillas, topped with cheddar cheese.

Nutrition: Calories: 266 Fat: 4.5g, Fiber: 11.91g, Carbs: 43.5g, Protein: 11.5g

25.   Greek Kafta Kabobs

Preparation Time: 15 minutes

Cooking Time: 10 minutes

Servings: 14

Ingredients: :

- One tablespoon coriander seed
- 1 tablespoon cumin seeds
- 1 teaspoon peppercorns
- 1 teaspoon allspice
- 1/2 teaspoon cardamom seeds
- 1/2 teaspoon turmeric powder
- 1 tablespoon oil
- 453 g 85% ground beef
- 32 g parsley
- One tablespoon minced garlic

Directions: :

1. Grind the seeds and peppercorns into powder and combine with the turmeric and allspice.
2. Put altogether of the Ingredients together in a blender and blend until well mixed.
3. Divide the meat into four equal parts and form a sausage around the skewers.
4. Cook in the air fryer at 370 degrees for 10 minutes.

Nutrition: Calories: 255 Fiber: 0.7 g, Fat: 11 g Carbs: 2.6 g, Protein: 35.1 g.

26. Classic Beef Ribs

Preparation Time: 35 minutes

Cooking Time: 25-30 minutes

Servings: 8

Ingredients: :

- 2 kg beef back ribs
- 1 tablespoon sunflower oil
- 1/2 teaspoon mixed peppercorns, cracked
- 1 teaspoon red pepper flakes
- 1 teaspoon dry mustard
- 1 tablespoon Coarse sea salt, to taste

Directions: :

5. Trim the excess fat from the beef ribs. Mix the sunflower oil, cracked peppercorns, red pepper, dry mustard, and salt. Rub over the ribs. Cook in the preheated air fryer at 395 degrees f for 11 minutes Turn the heat to 330 degrees f and continue to cook for 18 minutes more. Serve warm.

Nutrition: Calories: 310 Fat: 8.5g, Fiber: 11.1g Carbs: 45.9g Protein: 12.5g

27. Spicy Short Ribs in Red Wine Reduction

Preparation Time: **3 hrs.**

Cooking Time: 20 minutes

Servings: 6

Ingredients: :

- 1 ½ kg short ribs,
- 128 g red wine
- 64 g tamari sauce
- 1 lemon, juiced
- 1 teaspoon fresh ginger, grated
- 1 teaspoon salt
- 1 teaspoon black pepper
- 1 teaspoon paprika
- 1 teaspoon chipotle chili powder,
- 128 g ketchup
- 1 teaspoon garlic powder,
- 1 teaspoon cumin

Directions: :

6. In a ceramic bowl, place the beef ribs, wine, tamari sauce, lemon juice, ginger, salt, black pepper, paprika, and chipotle chili powder. Cover and let it marinate for 3 hours in the refrigerator. Discard the marinade and add the short ribs to the air fryer basket. Cook in the preheated air fry at 380 degrees f for 10 minutes, turning them over halfway through the cooking time. In the meantime, heat the saucepan over medium heat; add the reserved marinade and stir in the ketchup, garlic powder, and cumin. Cook until the sauce has thickened slightly. Pour the sauce over the warm ribs and serve immediately. Bon appétit!

Nutrition: Calories: 310 Fat: 9.5g, Fiber: 12.1g Carbs: 43.7g Protein: 15.g

28. Holiday Beef Roast

Preparation Time: 10 minutes
Cooking Time: 8 hours
Servings: 2
Ingredients: :

- 453 g bottom round roast
- 1/2 teaspoon oregano, dried
- 1/2 teaspoon rosemary, crushed
- 1/2 teaspoon fennel seed
- 1 teaspoon garlic, sliced
- 32 g water - 32 g onions, caramelized
- 1/2 teaspoon pepper
- 1/4 teaspoon salt

Directions: :

1. In a bowl, combine together rosemary, fennel seeds, pepper, oregano, and salt.
2. Rub rosemary mixture all over meat and place in the refrigerator for 30 minutes.
3. Place marinated roast into the inner pot of air fryer duo crisp and top with garlic, onions, and water.
4. Seal the pot with pressure cooking lid and select slow cook mode and cook on low for 8 hours.
5. Remove roast from pot and slice.
6. Serve and enjoy.

Nutrition: Calories: 425 Fat: 21.5g, Fiber: 19.5g Carbs: 39.5g Protein: 29.5g

29. Steak A La Mushrooms

Preparation Time: 10 minutes

Cooking Time: 18 minutes

Serving: 2

Ingredients: :

- 453 gSteaks, cubed
- 800g Mushrooms washed and halved
- 2 tablespoons butter, melted
- 1 teaspoon Worcestershire sauce
- 1/2 teaspoon garlic powder, optional
- pounds Salt, to taste
- pounds Fresh cracked black pepper, to taste
- Minced parsley, garnish

Directions: :

1. Toss the steak cubes with mushrooms, melted butter, garlic powder, salt, black, Worcestershire sauce, black pepper, and salt in a bowl.
2. Place the Air Fryer Basket in the Air fryer Duo.
3. Spread the steak cubes and mushrooms in the basket.
4. Put on the Air frying lid and seal it.
5. Hit the "Air fryer Button" and select 18 minutes of cooking time, then press "Start."
6. Once the Air fryer Duo beeps, remove its lid.
7. Garnish with parsley. Serve.

Nutrition: Calories: 423 Fat: 17.4g Fiber: 22.1g, Carbs: 37g Protein: 27.1g

30. Smoked Crispy Ribs

Preparation Time: 10 minutes

Cooking Time: 50 minutes

Serving: 2

Ingredients: :

- 1 rack of pork ribs
- 64 g broth
- 3 tablespoons Liquid Smoke
- 128 g Barbecue Sauce

Directions: :

1. Rub the rib rack with spice rub generously.
2. Pour the liquid into the Air fryer Duo Crisp.
3. Set an Air Fryer Basket into the Pot and place the rib rack in the basket.
4. Put on the pressure-cooking lid and seal it.
5. Hit the "Pressure Button" and select 30 minutes of cooking time, then press "Start."
6. Once the Air fryer Duo beeps, do a quick release and remove its lid.
7. Remove the ribs and rub them with barbecue sauce.
8. Empty the pot and place the Air Fryer Basket in it.
9. Set the ribs in the basket, and Air fry them for 20 minutes. Serve.

Nutrition: Calories: 341, Fat: 14.9g, Fiber: 21.5g, Carbs: 34.7g, Protein: 28.5g

31. Basic Taco Meat

Preparation Time: 5 minutes

Cooking Time: 10 minutes

Servings: 8

Ingredients: :

- 2 kg of ground beef
- ½ of a kg of diced onion
- ½ of a kg of diced bell pepper
- 128 g of tomato sauce (unsalted)
- 3 tablespoons of taco seasoning

Directions: :

1. Put the meat inside your cooker set to sauté. Brown the meat thoroughly and turn off the sautéing.
2. Add the rest of the Ingredients into the meat and stir them together.
3. Using the manual setting set the timer for 8 minutes.
4. After the beep, you can either release the pressure quickly or let it release naturally. Serve with the garnishes of your choice, for example over some cauliflower rice.

Nutrition: Calories: 201, Fat: 11.4g, Fiber: 7.1g, Carbs: 21.4g, Protein: 20.1g

32.   Tangy Beef Steak

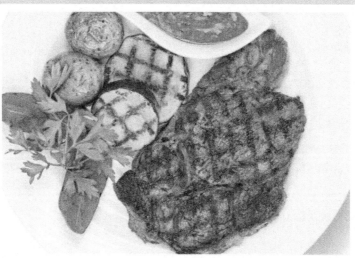

5 minutes

40 minutes

4

- 4 medium beef steaks
- 3 garlic cloves; minced
- 128 g balsamic vinegar
- 2 tbsp. olive oil
- 1 tbsp. Salt and black pepper to taste.

1. Take a bowl and mix steaks with the rest of the Ingredients and toss.
2. Transfer the steaks to your air fryer's basket and cook at 390°F for 35 minutes, flipping them halfway
3. Divide among plates and serve with a side salad.

Calories: 276, Fat: 10.5g, Fiber: 4.1g, Carbs: 9.7g, Protein: 19.4g

33.   Ginger-Orange Beef Strips

Preparation Time: 5 minutes

Cooking Time: 25 minutes

Servings: 3

Ingredients: :

- 1 ½ kg stir fry steak slices
- 1 ½ teaspoon sesame oil
- One navel orange, segmented
- One tablespoon olive oil
- One tablespoon rice vinegar
- One teaspoon grated ginger
- Two scallions, chopped
- Three cloves of garlic, minced
- Three tablespoons molasses
- Three tablespoons soy sauce
- Six tablespoons cornstarch

Directions: :

1. Preheat the air fryer to 3300F.
2. Season the steak slices with soy sauce and dust with cornstarch.
3. Place in the air fryer basket and cook for 25 minutes.
4. Meanwhile, place in the skillet oil and heat over medium flame.
5. Sauté the garlic and ginger until fragrant.
6. Stir in the oranges, molasses, and rice vinegar. Season with salt and pepper to taste.
7. Once the meat is cooked, place in the skillet and stir to coat the sauce.
8. Drizzle with oil and garnish with scallions

Nutrition: Calories per serving: 306, Carbs: 43.6g, Protein: 9.4g, Fat: 10.4g , Fiber: 12.5g

34. Pub Burgers

Preparation Time: 30 minutes
Cooking Time: 30 minutes
Servings: 8
Ingredients: :

- 2-kg ground beef
- 3 green onions, chopped
- 1 tbsp. ketchup
- 8 slices American cheese
- 8 Burger Buns, split
- 1/2 tsp. salt
- 1/4 tsp. pepper
- ¾-kg can chicken gumbo soup partially drained
- ¾-kg tomato soup - 2 tbsp. mustard

Directions: :

1. Select Sauté on normal.
2. Cook ground beef until no longer pink.
3. Put in the rest of the Ingredients except for cheese and bun to Air fryer. Cook on High Pressure with Manual mode for 7 minutes. Spoon beef mixture onto buns.
4. Add cheese slices to serve.

Nutrition: Calories: 315 Fat: 12.6g, Fiber: 4.6g Carbs: 45.1g Protein: 19.1g

35. Mediterranean Turkey Burgers

Preparation Time: 30 minutes

Cooking Time: 16-18 minutes

Servings: 4

Ingredients: :

- 453 g ground turkey
- 64 g breadcrumbs
- 32 g Parmesan cheese, grated
- 1 egg, beaten - 1 tbsp minced garlic
- 1 tbsp olive oil
- 1 tsp horseradish sauce
- 4 tbsp Greek yogurt
- 4 buns, halved - 4 tomato slices

Directions: :

1. Preheat air fryer to 380 F. Grease the air fryer basket with cooking spray.

2. In a bowl, combine ground turkey, breadcrumbs, Parmesan cheese, egg, garlic, salt, and black pepper. Mix well. Form balls and flatten to make patties. Brush them with olive oil and place in the air fryer.

3. Air Fry for 16-18 minutes, flipping once halfway through until nice and golden. Mix the yogurt with horseradish sauce. Assemble the burgers by spreading the yogurt mixture, then the patties, and finally top with fresh tomato slices. Serve immediately.

Nutrition: Calories: 231 Fat: 7.5g, Fiber: 11.1g Carbs: 54g Protein: 12.1g

36. Beef and Blue Cheese Burgers

Preparation Time: 15 minutes

Cooking Time: 20 minutes

Servings: 4

Ingredients: :

- 1 tbsp Olive oil - 453 glean ground beef
- 64 g blue cheese, crumbled
- 1 teaspoon Worcestershire sauce
- ½ teaspoon freshly ground black pepper
- ½ teaspoon hot sauce
- ½ teaspoon minced garlic
- ¼ teaspoon salt - 4 whole-wheat buns

Directions: :

1. Set to 360F. Spray a fryer basket lightly with olive oil.
2. In a large bowl, mix together the beef, blue cheese, Worcestershire sauce, pepper, hot sauce, garlic, and salt.
3. Form the mixture into 4 patties. Place the patties in the fryer basket in a single layer, leaving a little room between them for even cooking. Air fry for 10 minutes. Flip over and cook until the meat reaches an internal temperature of at least 160°F, an additional 7 to 10 minutes. Place each patty on a bun and serve with low-calorie toppings like sliced tomatoes or onions.

Nutrition: Calories: 321 Fat: 15.4g, Fiber: 14g Carbs: 51.5g Protein: 14.5g

37.   Hoisin Turkey Burgers

Preparation Time: 40 minutes

Cooking Time: 20 minutes

Servings: 4

Ingredients: :

- 1 tbsp Olive oil
- 453 g lean ground turkey
- 32 g whole-wheat bread crumbs
- 32 g hoisin sauce
- 2 tablespoons soy sauce
- 4 whole-wheat buns

Directions: :

1. Set to 360 F. Spray a fryer basket lightly with olive oil.
2. In a large bowl, mix together the turkey, bread crumbs, hoisin sauce, and soy sauce.
3. Form the mixture into 4 equal patties. Cover with plastic wrap and refrigerate the patties for 30 minutes.
4. Place the patties in the fryer basket in a single layer. Spray the patties lightly with olive oil.
5. Air fry for 10 minutes. Flip the patties over, lightly spray with olive oil, and cook until golden brown, an additional 5 to 10 minutes.
6. Place the patties on buns and top with your choice of low-calorie burger toppings like sliced tomatoes, onions, and cabbage slaw.

Nutrition: Calories: 342 Fat: 10.6g, Fiber: 14g Carbs: 41.7g Protein: 10.6g

38.   Herbed Pork Burgers

Preparation Time: 30 minutes
Cooking Time: 45 minutes
Servings: 8
Ingredients: :

- 2 small onions, chopped
- 600g ground pork
- 2 teaspoons fresh basil, chopped
- 8 burger buns
- 64 g cheddar cheese, grated
- 2 teaspoons mustard
- 2 teaspoons garlic puree
- 2 teaspoons tomato puree
- 1 tbsp Salt and freshly ground black pepper, to taste
- 2 teaspoons dried mixed herbs, crushed

Directions: :

1. Preheat the Air fryer to 395 o F and grease an Air fryer basket.
2. Mix all the Ingredients in a bowl except cheese and buns.
3. Make 8 equal-sized patties from the pork mixture and arrange thee patties in the Air fryer basket.
4. Cook for about 45 minutes, flipping once in between and arrange the patties in buns with cheese to serve.

Nutrition: Calories: 290 Fat: 17.5g Fiber: 9.5gg, Carbs: 67.9g Protein: 17.7g

39.   Korean Burgers

Preparation Time: 40 minutes

Cooking Time: 15 minutes

Servings: 4

Ingredients: :

- (453.59 g) Lean Ground Beef
- 2 tablespoons of gochujang
- 1 tablespoon of dark soy sauce
- 2 teaspoons Minced Garlic
- 2 teaspoons of minced ginger
- 2 teaspoons of Sugar
- 1 tablespoon of Sesame Oil
- 32 g of Green Onions
- 1/2 tsp (0.5 tsp) of Salt
- For the Gochujang Mayonnaise
- 32 g Mayonnaise
- 1 tablespoon of gochujang
- 1 tablespoon of Sesame Oil
- 2 teaspoons of Sesame Seeds
- 32 g of scallions, chopped
- 4 hamburger buns for serving

Directions: :

1. In a large bowl, mix the ground beef, gochujang, soy sauce, garlic, ginger, sugar, sesame oil, chopped onions, and salt and allow the mixture to rest in a fridge for 30 minutes or up to 24 hours.

2. Divide the meat into four portions and form round patties with a slight depression in the middle to prevent the burgers from blowing out in a dome-shaped cooking process.

3. Set your air fryer for 10 minutes at 360F, and put the patties in the air fryer basket in a single layer.

4. Make sure the Gochujang Mayonnaise: combines together the sesame oil, mayonnaise, gochujang, sesame seeds, and scallions when cooking the patties.

Nutrition: Calories: 398 Fat: 10.6g, Fiber: 12.9g Carbs: 56.8g, Protein: 15.8g

40.   Orange Turkey Burgers

Preparation Time: 20 minutes

Cooking Time: 11-15 minutes

Servings: 4

Ingredients: :

- Ground Turkey – 1 pound
- Ground mustard seed – 1 teaspoon
- Grape nuts Nuggets – 1 tablespoon
- Chinese Five Spice - ¼ teaspoon
- Diced scallion – 1
- Orange Basting Sauce:
- Orange Marmalade – 40g
- Soy sauce – 1 tablespoon
- Fish sauce – 1 teaspoon
- Oyster sauce – 2 teaspoons
- Orange Aioli:
- Orange juice – 1 tablespoon
- Orange zest – 1 teaspoon
- Mayonnaise – 50g
- Ground chili paste – 1 teaspoon

Directions: :

1. In a small bowl, whisk Orange Aioli Ingredients and refrigerate.
2. In another bowl combine basting sauce and keep aside.
3. Set the air fryer at 200 degrees Celsius and pre-heat for about 10 minutes.
4. In a medium bowl combine the burger Ingredients and add 1 tablespoon of basting sauce.
5. Shape the mix into 6 patties and create an indentation at the center of the patties.
6. Now slightly grease the surface of air fryer basket with cooking oil and place the patties in the frying basket.
7. Set the temperature at 180 degrees Celsius and cook for 9 minutes.
8. Flip the burgers intermittently every 4 minutes.
9. Baste burger after every 2 minutes.
10. After 9 minutes of cooking, baste the burger and cook a further 3 minutes.
11. Serve hot along with Orange Aioli.

Nutrition: Calories: 410 Fat: 6.5g, Fiber: 13.8g Carbs: 45.6, Protein: 19.5 g

41.   Marinated Rib Eye Steak

Preparation Time: 10 minutes

Cooking Time: 20 minutes

Servings: 4

Ingredients: :

- 2 kg rib eye steak
- 1 tbsp Salt and dark pepper to the taste
- 1 tablespoons olive oil
- For the rib:
- 3 tablespoons sweet paprika
- 2 tablespoons onion powder
- 2 tablespoons garlic powder
- 1 tablespoon dark colored sugar
- 2 tablespoons oregano, dried
- 1 tablespoon cumin, ground
- 1 tablespoon rosemary, dried

Directions: :

1. In a bowl, blend paprika in with onion and garlic powder, sugar, oregano, rosemary, salt, pepper and cumin, mix and rub steak with this blend.
2. Season steak with salt and pepper, rub again with the oil, put in the air fryer cooker and cook at 400 Deg. Fahrenheit for about 20 minutes, flipping them midway.
3. Transfer steak to a cutting board, cut and present with a side plate of mixed greens. Enjoy the recipe

Nutrition: Calories: 451, Fat: 14g, Fiber: 12.1g, Carbs: 29.7g, Protein: 22.1g

42. Glazed Skirt Steak

Preparation Time: 10 minutes

Cooking Time: 15 minutes

Servings: 6

Ingredients: :

- 1¼ kg skirt steak
- 64 g low-Sodium soy sauce
- 32 g white wine
- 3-4 tablespoons fresh lemon juice
- 2 tablespoons sesame oil
- 3 tablespoons maple syrup
- 1 tablespoon red pepper flakes, crushed
- 2 garlic cloves, minced

Directions: :

1. In a large resealable bag, place all the Ingredients except for the scallions.
2. Seal the bag and shake to mix well.
3. Refrigerate for up to 2 hours.
4. Remove the steak from bag and set aside at room temperature for 20 minutes before Cooking.
5. Place the skirt steak onto a greased baking pan.
6. Arrange the drip pan in the bottom of the air fryer.
7. Place the baking pan over the drip pan.
8. Select "bake" and then adjust the temperature to 400 degrees f.
9. Set the timer for 10 minutes and press "start".
10. When the display shows "turn food" do nothing.
11. When Cooking time is complete, remove the baking pan from toaster oven.
12. Place the steak onto a cutting board for about 10-15 minutes before slicing.
13. With a sharp knife, cut the steak into desired size slices and serve.

Nutrition: Calories: 410, Fat: 14g, Fiber: 15.9g, Carbs: 21.6g, Protein: 22.8g

43.   Southern Pulled Pork

Preparation Time: 30 minutes

Cooking Time: 35 minutes

Servings: 4

Ingredients: :

- ½ Teaspoon Paprika - 1 Teaspoon Black Pepper
- 1 Tablespoon Chili Flakes
- 1 Teaspoon Cayenne Pepper
- 96 g Cream - 453 g Pork Tenderloin
- 1 Teaspoon Sea Salt, Fine - 512 g Chicken Stock
- 1 Teaspoon Thyme, Ground - 1 Teaspoon Butter

Directions: :

14. Place your chicken stock into your air fryer, and then get out your pork. Sprinkle it with black pepper, paprika, cayenne, salt and chili flakes. Heat your air fryer to 370, and then cook for twenty minutes. Strain your liquid, and then shred your meat. Add your butter and cream to the mix, and then cook at 360 for four minutes. Allow it to cool before serving.

Nutrition: Calories: 271 Fat:10.5g, Fiber: 11g Carbs: 12.9g, Protein: 19.5 g

44. Dijon Lime Chicken

Preparation Time: 20 minutes

Cooking Time: 35 minutes

Servings: 2

Ingredients: :

- Chicken drumsticks – 4
- Dried parsley – ½ tsp.
- Black pepper – ¼ tsp.
- Lime juice – ½
- Garlic clove – 1, minced
- Mayonnaise – ½ tbsp.
- Dijon mustard – 1 ½ tbsps.
- 1 tablespoon Salt, to taste

Directions: :

15. Add chicken drumsticks into the large mixing bowl. Add remaining Ingredients over chicken and toss until well coated. Add chicken drumsticks into the multi-level air fryer basket and place basket into the air fryer. Seal pot with air fryer lid. Select bake mode and cook at 380 F for 35 minutes. Serve.

Nutrition: Calories: 241, Fat: 3.4g, Fiber: 6.1g, Carbs: 31.7g, Protein: 13.4 g

45. Parmesan Chicken Nuggets

Preparation Time: 30 minutes

Cooking Time: 30 minutes

Servings: 4

Ingredients: :

- Chicken breasts – 1kg pounds, cut into chunks
- Garlic powder – ½ tsp.
- Parmesan cheese – 6 tbsps., shredded
- Mayonnaise – 32 g
- Salt – ½ tsp.

Directions: :

16. Line the multi-level air fryer basket with parchment paper and set aside. In a medium bowl, mix together mayonnaise, shredded cheese, garlic powder, and salt. Coat chicken chunks with the mayo mixture and place into the air fryer basket and place the basket into the air fryer. Seal pot with the air fryer lid. Select bake mode and cook at 380 F for 25-30 minutes. Serve.

Nutrition: Calories: 197, Fat: 2.6g, Fiber: 5.1g, Carbs: 26.7g, Protein: 8.5g

46. Garlic Honey Chicken

Preparation Time: 10 minutes

Cooking Time: 20-30 minutes

Servings: 4

Ingredients: :

- 900ml water
- 32 g low sodium soy sauce
- 32 g honey
- 2 cloves garlic, minced
- ¼ tsp. black pepper
- 1/2-kg medium-size boneless skinless chicken breasts
- 2 tsp. cornstarch

Directions: :

1. Combine water, soy sauce, honey, garlic, chicken, and pepper in Air fryer.
2. Cook at High Pressure for 10 minutes.
3. In a bowl, mix 2 teaspoons cornstarch and 1 tablespoon water.
4. Cook cornstarch mixture on Sauté mode for 2-3 minutes.
5. Dip sliced chicken in sauce.
6. Serve with rice and vegetable.

Nutrition: Calories: 267, Fat: 8.5g, Fiber: 7.1g, Carbs: 31.2g, Protein: 12.6 g

47. Chicken Sausage with Nestled Eggs

Preparation Time: 20 minutes

Cooking Time: 17 minutes

Servings: 6

Ingredients: :

- 6 eggs
- 2 bell peppers, seeded and sliced
- 1 teaspoon dried oregano
- 1 teaspoon hot paprika
- 1 teaspoon freshly cracked black pepper
- 6 chicken sausages
- 1 teaspoon sea salt
- 1/2 shallots, cut into wedges
- 1 teaspoon dried basil

Directions: :

1. Take four ramekins and divide chicken sausages, shallot, and bell pepper among those ramekins. Cook at 315 degrees f for about 12 minutes.

2. Now, crack an egg into each ramekin. Sprinkle the eggs with hot paprika, basil, oregano, salt, and cracked black pepper. Cook for 5 more minutes at 405 degrees f.

Nutrition: Calories: 314, Fat: 18.4g, Fiber: 19.8g, Carbs: 27g, Protein: 19.1g

48. Thai Chicken Satay

Preparation Time: 20 minutes
Cooking Time: 20-30 minutes
Servings: 12
Ingredients: :

- 64 g crunchy peanut butter
- 42 g chicken broth
- 3 tablespoons low-sodium soy sauce
- 2 tablespoons lemon juice
- 2 cloves garlic, minced
- 2 tablespoons olive oil
- 1 teaspoon curry powder
- 453 g chicken tenders

Directions: :

1. Set to 390 Grill. In a medium bowl, combine the peanut butter, chicken broth, soy sauce, lemon juice, garlic, olive oil, and curry powder, and mix well with a wire whisk until smooth. Remove 2 tablespoons of this mixture to a small bowl. Put remaining sauce into a serving bowl and set aside.

2. Add the chicken tenders to the bowl with the 2 tablespoons sauce and stir to coat. Let stand for a few minutes to marinate, then run a bamboo skewer through each chicken tender lengthwise.

3. Put the chicken in the air fryer basket and cook in batches for 6 to 9 minutes or until the chicken reaches 165°F on a meat thermometer. Serve the chicken with the reserved sauce.

Nutrition: Calories: 299, Fat: 7.5g, Fiber: 8.1g, Carbs:29.5g, Protein: 12.4 g

49. Sweet and Sour Chicken

Preparation Time: 15 minutes

Cooking Time: 20-30 minutes

Servings: 6

Ingredients: :

- 6 chicken drumsticks
- 3 tablespoons lemon juice, divided
- 3 tablespoons low-sodium soy sauce, divided
- 1 tablespoon peanut oil
- 3 tablespoons honey
- 3 tablespoons brown sugar
- 2 tablespoons ketchup
- 32 g pineapple juice

Directions: :

1. Set to 350 Bake. Sprinkle the drumsticks with 1 tablespoon of lemon juice and 1 tablespoon of soy sauce. Place in the air fryer basket and drizzle with the peanut oil. Toss to coat. Bake for 18 minutes or until the chicken is almost done.

2. Meanwhile, in a 6-inch bowl combine the remaining 2 tablespoons of lemon juice, the remaining 2 tablespoons of soy sauce, honey, brown sugar, ketchup, and pineapple juice.

3. Add the cooked chicken to the bowl and stir to coat the chicken well with the sauce.

4. Place the metal bowl in the basket. Cook for 5 to 7 minutes or until the chicken is glazed and registers 165°F on a meat thermometer.

Nutrition: Calories: 277, Fat: 12.5g, Fiber: 10.9g, Carbs: 31.9g, Protein: 12g

50. Thanksgiving Turkey with Mustard Gravy

Preparation Time: 50 minutes

Cooking Time: 45 minutes

Servings: 6

Ingredients: :

- 2 teaspoons butter, softened
- 1 teaspoon dried sage
- 2 sprigs rosemary, chopped
- 1 teaspoon salt
- 1/4 teaspoon freshly ground black pepper, or more to taste
- 1 whole turkey breast
- 2 tablespoons turkey broth
- 2 tablespoons whole-grain mustard
- 1 tablespoon butter

Directions: :

1. Start by preheating your air fryer to 360 degrees f.
2. To make the rub, combine 2 tablespoons of butter, sage, rosemary, salt, and pepper; mix well to combine and spread it evenly over the surface of the turkey breast.
3. Roast for 20 minutes in an air fryer cooking basket. Flip the turkey breast over and cook for a further 15 to 16 minutes. Now, flip it back over and roast for 12 minutes more.
4. While the turkey is roasting, whisk the other Ingredients in a saucepan. After that, spread the gravy all over the turkey breast.
5. Let the turkey rest for a few minutes before carving.

Nutrition: Calories: 415, Fat: 19.4g, Fiber: 12.1g, Carbs: 31g, Protein: 27.1g

51. Butter and Orange Fried Chicken

Preparation Time: 20 minutes

Cooking Time: 13 minutes

Servings: 4

Ingredients: :

- ½ tablespoon Worcestershire sauce
- 1 teaspoon finely grated orange zest
- 2 tablespoons melted butter
- ½ teaspoon smoked paprika
- 4 chicken drumsticks, rinsed and halved
- 1 teaspoon sea salt flakes
- 1 tablespoon cider vinegar
- 1/2 teaspoon mixed peppercorns, freshly cracked

Directions: :

1. Firstly, pat the chicken drumsticks dry. Coat them with the melted butter on all sides. Toss the chicken drumsticks with the other Ingredients.
2. Transfer them to the air fryer cooking basket and roast for about 13 minutes at 345 degrees f.

Nutrition: Calories: 314, Fat: 11.4g, Fiber: 12.1g, Carbs: 29.7g, Protein: 24.1g

52.   Chicken Alfredo

Preparation Time: 15 minutes

Cooking Time: 15-20 minutes

Servings: 4

Ingredients: :

- 453 g chicken breasts, skinless and boneless
- ½kg button mushrooms, sliced
- 1 medium-sized onion, chopped
- 1 tablespoon olive oil
- 256 g cooked rice
- 1 jar (100g) Alfredo sauce
- 1 tablespoon Salt and pepper to taste
- ½ teaspoon thyme, dried

Directions: :

1. Cut the chicken breasts into 1-inch cubes. Mix chicken, onion, and mushrooms in a large bowl. Season with salt and dried thyme and mix well. Preheat your air fryer to 370°Fahrenheit and sprinkle basket with olive oil. Transfer chicken and vegetables to fryer and cook for 12-minutes and stir occasionally. Stir in the Alfredo sauce. Cook for another 4-minutes. Serve with cooked rice

Nutrition: Calories: 280, Fat: 10.5g, Fiber: 8.5g, Carbs: 44.1g, Protein: 12.9 g

53. Turkey Loaf

Preparation Time: 20 minutes

Cooking Time: 40 minutes

Servings: 4

Ingredients: :

- 1 egg
- ½ teaspoon dried savory dill
- 168 g walnuts, finely chopped
- 1 ½.kg turkey breast, diced
- ½ teaspoon ground allspice
- ¼ teaspoon black pepper
- 1 garlic clove, minced
- 1 tablespoon Dijon mustard
- 1 tablespoon liquid Aminos
- 1 tablespoon tomato paste
- 2 tablespoons parmesan cheese, grated
- 1 tablespoon onion flakes

Directions: :

1. Preheat your air fryer to 375°Fahrenheit. Grease a baking dish using cooking spray. Whisk dill, egg, tomato paste, liquid aminos, mustard, garlic, allspice, salt, and pepper. Mix well and add diced turkey. Mix again and add cheese, walnuts and onion flakes. Put mixture into baking dish and bake for 40-minutes in air fryer. Serve hot!

Nutrition: Calories: 277, Fat: 5.7g, Fiber: 4.51g, Carbs: 45.6g, Protein: 10.6 g

54.　Cheesy Turkey Calzone

Preparation Time: 20 minutes

Cooking Time: 10-15minutes

Servings: 4

Ingredients: :

- 1 free-range egg, beaten
- 32 g mozzarella cheese, grated
- 128 g cheddar cheese, grated
- 1-kg bacon, diced, cooked
- 1kg Cooked turkey, shredded
- 4 tablespoons tomato sauce
- 1 tablespoon Salt and pepper to taste
- 1 teaspoon thyme
- 1 teaspoon basil
- 1 teaspoon oregano
- 1 package frozen pizza dough

Directions: :

1. Roll the pizza dough out into small circles, the same size as a small pizza. Add thyme, oregano, basil into a bowl with tomato sauce and mix well. Pour a small amount of sauce onto your pizza bases and spread across the surface. Add the turkey, bacon, and cheese. Brush the edge of dough with beaten egg, then fold over and pinch to seal. Brush the outside with more egg. Place into air fryer and cook at 350°Fahrenehit for 10-minutes. Serve warm.

Nutrition: Calories: 265 Fat: 8.5g, Fiber: 7.1g Carbs: 39.7g Protein: 12.5 g

55. Mozzarella Turkey Rolls

Preparation Time: 15 minutes

Cooking Time: 10-15 minutes

Servings: 4

Ingredients: :

- 4 slices turkey breast
- 4 chive shoots (for tying rolls)
- 1 tomato, sliced
- 64 g basil, fresh, chopped
- 128 g mozzarella, sliced

Directions: :

1. Preheat your air fryer to 390°Fahrenheit. Place the slices of mozzarella cheese, tomato, and basil onto each slice of turkey. Roll up and tie with chive shoot. Place into air fryer and cook for 10-minutes. Serve warm.

Nutrition: Calories: 245, Fat: 5.7g, Fiber: 9.1g, Carbs: 28.6g, Protein: 12.8 g

56. Curry Chicken Wings

Preparation Time: 30 minutes

Cooking Time: 20 minutes

Servings: 4

Ingredients: :

- 128 g rice milk
- 1 tbsp soy sauce
- 1 tbsp red curry paste
- 1 tbsp sugar
- 8 chicken wings
- 2 tbsp fresh parsley, chopped

Directions: :

1. Preheat air fryer to 380 F.
2. In a bowl, mix all the Ingredients, except for the parsley. Marinate for 20 minutes. Grease the air fryer basket with cooking spray. After 20 minutes, drain the wings and reserve the marinade.
3. Place wings in the frying basket and Air Fry for 18-20 minutes, flipping once. Add the marinade to a saucepan over medium heat, and cook until thickened, 8 minutes. Pour this sauce over the chicken and top with parsley to serve

Nutrition: Calories: 212 Fat: 4.5g, Fiber: 9.4g, Carbs: 23.8g, Protein: 10.4g

57.   Roasted Duck Breasts with Endives

Preparation Time: 20 minutes

Cooking Time: 35 minutes

Servings: 4

Ingredients: :

- duck breasts 2 - sugar-1 tbsp.
- Salt and black pepper to the taste
- olive oil-1 tbsp. - endives; julienned-6
- cranberries-2 tbsp. - White wine-224 g
- Garlic; minced-1 tbsp.

Directions: :

1. Score duck bosoms and season them with salt and pepper, place in preheated air fryer and cook at 350 °F, for 20 minutes; flipping them midway.
2. On the other hand; heat a skillet with the oil over medium warmth, include sugar and endives; blend and cook for 2 minutes. Include salt, pepper, wine, garlic, cream, and cranberries; blend and cook for 3 minutes.
3. Divide duck bosoms on plates; spread the endives sauce all finished and serve.

Nutrition: Calories: 314 Fat: 18.4g, Fiber: 15.1g Carbs: 31g Protein: 29 g

58. Coconut Curry Pork Roast

Preparation Time: 15 minutes

Cooking Time: 60 minutes

Servings: 6

Ingredients: :

- ½ teaspoon curry powder
- ½ teaspoon ground turmeric powder
- 1 can unsweetened coconut milk
- 1 tablespoons Sugar
- 2 tablespoons fish sauce
- 2 tablespoons soy sauce
- 3 kg pork shoulder
- 1 tablespoon Salt and pepper to taste

Directions: :

1. Place all Ingredients in bowl and allow the meat to marinate in the fridge for at least 2 hours.
2. Preheat the air fryer to 390°f.
3. Place the grill pan accessory in the air fryer.
4. Grill the meat for 20 minutes making sure to flip the pork every 10 minutes for even grilling and cook in batches.
5. Meanwhile, pour the marinade in a saucepan and allow to simmer for 10 minutes until the sauce thickens.
6. Baste the pork with the sauce before serving.

Nutrition: Calories: 415, Fat: 16.6g, Fiber: 14.1g, Carbs: 31.7g, Protein: 22.1g

59.   Chinese Pork Dumplings

Preparation Time: 20 minutes

Cooking Time: 15 minutes

Servings: 8

Ingredients: :

- ¼ teaspoon crushed red pepper
- ½ teaspoon Sugar
- 1 tablespoon chopped fresh ginger
- 1 tablespoon chopped garlic
- 1 teaspoon canola oil
- 1 teaspoon toasted sesame oil
- 18 dumpling wrappers
- 2 tablespoons rice vinegar
- 2 teaspoons soy sauce
- 512 g bok choy, chopped
- 112 g ground pork

Directions: :

1. Heat oil in a skillet and sauté the ginger and garlic until fragrant. Stir in the ground pork and cook for 5 minutes.
2. Stir in the bok choy and crushed red pepper. Season with salt and pepper to taste. Allow to cool.
3. Place the meat mixture in the middle of the dumpling wrappers. Fold the wrappers to seal the meat mixture in.
4. Place the bok choy in the grill pan.
5. Cook the dumplings in the air fryer at 330°f for 15 minutes.
6. Meanwhile, prepare the dipping sauce by combining the remaining Ingredients in a bowl.

Nutrition: Calories: 399, Fat: 10.5g, Fiber: 9.5g, Carbs: 31.4g, Protein: 19.3g

60. Five Spicy Crispy Roasted Pork

Preparation Time: 20 minutes

Cooking Time: 35 minutes

Servings: 6

Ingredients: :

- 1 teaspoon Chinese five spice powder
- 1 teaspoon white pepper
- 2 kg pork belly
- 2 teaspoons garlic salt

Directions: :

1. Preheat the air fryer oven to 390°f.
2. Mix all the spices in a bowl to create the dry rub.
3. Score the skin of the pork belly with a knife and season the entire pork with the spice rub.
4. Place in the air fryer basket and cook for 40 to 45 minutes until the skin is crispy.
5. Chop before serving.

Nutrition: Calories: 439 Fat: 18.5g, Fiber: 14.3g Carbs: 22.9g Protein: 28g

61. Tuscan Pork Chops

Preparation Time: 20 minutes

Cooking Time: 10-15 minutes

Servings: 4

Ingredients: :

- 32 g all-purpose flour
- 1 teaspoon salt
- 3/4 teaspoons seasoned pepper
- 4 (1-inch-thick) boneless pork chops
- 1 tablespoon olive oil
- 3 to 4 garlic cloves
- 96 g balsamic vinegar
- 96 g chicken broth
- 3 plum tomatoes, seeded and diced
- 2 Tablespoons capers

Directions: :

1. Combine flour, salt, and pepper
2. Press pork chops into flour mixture on both sides until evenly covered.
3. Cook in your air fryer oven at 360 degrees for 14 minutes, flipping halfway through.
4. While the pork chops cook, warm olive oil in a medium skillet.
5. Add garlic and sauté for 1 minute; then mix in vinegar and chicken broth.
6. Add capers and tomatoes and turn to high heat.
7. Bring the sauce to a boil, stirring regularly, then add pork chops, Cooking for one minute.
8. Remove from heat and cover for about 5 minutes to allow the pork to absorb some of the sauce; serve hot.

Nutrition: Calories: 391 Fat: 14.9g, Fiber: 15.3gg Carbs: 28.5g, Protein: 24.9g

62. Pork Carnitas

Preparation Time: 20 minutes

Cooking Time: 35-40 minutes

Servings: 12

Ingredients: :

- 1kg skinless, boneless pork shoulder, chopped into 2-inch chunks
- 64 g orange juice
- 1 tsp. ground cumin
- 1 cinnamon stick
- 1 tbsp. dried oregano
- 1/2 tsp. ground cloves
- 2 1/2 tsp. kosher salt
- 12 tortillas
- 2 tsp. ancho chili powder
- 1 onion, quartered
- 3 jalapeños, halved
- 6 cloves garlic
- 2 tsp. black pepper

Directions: :

1. Put all Ingredients except tortillas into Air fryer.
2. Cook on High Pressure for 35 minutes.
3. Discard spices.
4. Shred meat.
5. Pour 96 g cooking liquid over pork.
6. Broil until deeply browned in spots.
7. Serve with tortillas, thinly sliced cabbage, pickled red onion, sour cream, and hot sauce.

Nutrition: Calories: 287 Fat: 12.9g, Fiber: 7.7g Carbs: 31.4g Protein: 18 g

63.   Country Style Ribs

Preparation Time: 10 minutes

Cooking Time: 15-20 minutes

Servings: 4

Ingredients: :

- 4 country-style pork ribs, trimmed of excess fat
- 1 tablespoon Salt and black pepper to taste
- 1 teaspoon dried marjoram
- 1 teaspoon garlic powder
- 1 teaspoon thyme
- 2 teaspoons dry mustard
- 3 tablespoons coconut oil
- 3 tablespoons cornstarch

Directions: :

8. Preheat the air fryer to 400°Fahrenheit for 2 minutes. Place Ingredients in a bowl, except pork ribs. Soak the ribs in the mixture and rub in. Place the ribs into air fryer for 12-minutes. Serve and enjoy!

Nutrition: Calories: 271, Fat: 10.5g Fiber: 8.5g, Carbs: 38.9g , Protein: 12.5 g

64. Crispy Pork Chops

Preparation Time: 15 minutes

Cooking Time: 15-20 minutes

Servings: 2

Ingredients: :

- 2 pork chops
- 64 g breadcrumbs
- 1 tablespoon olive oil
- 1 egg, beaten
- 1 tablespoon almond flour
- 1 tablespoon Salt and pepper to taste

Directions: :

9. Season pork chops with salt and pepper. Add flour to mixing bowl. In another small bowl, add beaten egg. In a third bowl, combine breadcrumbs with olive oil. Coat the pork chops with flour, dip in egg, and coat with breadcrumbs. Place chops into air fryer basket and cook at 400°Fahrenheit for 10-minutes. Flip chops over and cook on the other side for an additional 5-minutes. Serve warm.

Nutrition: Calories: 266, Fat: 10.9g, Fiber: 9.6g, Carbs: 29.5g, Protein: 10.9 g

65. Jamaican Meatballs

Preparation Time: 20 minutes

Cooking Time: 20 minutes

Servings: 4

Ingredients: :

- 2 tbsp Jerk Dry Rub
- 100g mince chicken
- 100g breadcrumbs
- 4 tbsp raw honey
- 1 tbsp soy sauce

Directions: :

1. In a bowl, place chicken and add breadcrumbs and 1 tbsp Jerk dry rub seasoning. Mix properly and press into meatball shapes, using a meatball press.
2. Place in the air fryer and cook at 180°C for 15 minutes.
3. In a mixing bowl, combine soy sauce, honey and remaining jerk seasoning and mix well.
4. When meatballs are done, dip or toss them in the sauce and serve.

Nutrition: Calories: 155, Fat: 4.1g, Fiber: 3.1g, Carbs: 21.7g, Protein: 9.7g

66.   Pork Chops in Lemon Sage Sauce

Preparation Time: 10 minutes

Cooking Time: 15 minutes

Servings: 2

Ingredients: :

- 2 pork chops
- 1 tablespoon Salt and black pepper to the taste
- 1 tablespoon olive oil
- 2 tablespoons butter
- 1 shallot, sliced
- 1 handful sage, chopped
- 1 teaspoon lemon juice

Directions: :

5. Season pork chops with salt and pepper, rub with the oil, put in your air fryer and cook at 370 degrees F for 10 minutes, flipping them halfway. Meanwhile, heat up a pan with the butter over medium heat, add shallot, stir and cook for 2 minutes. Add sage and lemon juice, stir well, cook for a few more minutes and take off heat. Divide pork chops on plates, drizzle sage sauce all over and serve. Enjoy!

Nutrition: Calories: 291 Fat: 6.9g, Fiber: 13.1g, Carbs: 34.6g, Protein: 13.8 g

67.   Sweet and Spicy Pork Chops

Preparation Time: 10 minutes

Cooking Time: 15 minutes

Servings: 4

Ingredients: :

- 1 tablespoon olive oil, plus more for spraying
- 3 tablespoons brown sugar
- ½ teaspoon cayenne pepper
- ½ teaspoon garlic powder
- ½ teaspoon salt
- ¼ teaspoon freshly ground black pepper
- 4 thin boneless pork chops, trimmed of excess fat

Directions: :

1. Set to 370 F Spray a fryer basket lightly with olive oil.
2. In a small bowl, mix together the brown sugar, 1 tablespoon of olive oil, cayenne pepper, garlic powder, salt, and black pepper.
3. Coat each pork chop with the marinade, shaking them to remove any excess, and place in the fryer basket in a single layer. You may need to cook them in batches.
4. Air fry for 7 minutes. Flip the pork chops over and brush with more marinade. Cook until the chops reach an internal temperature of 145°F, an additional 5 to 8 minutes.

Nutrition: Calories: 290 Fat: 12.6g, Fiber: 10.5g Carbs: 34.6g Protein: 12.4g

68.   Lime-Chili Pork Tenderloin

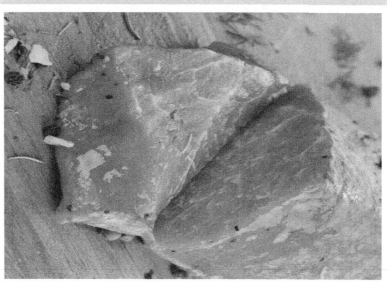

Preparation Time: 10 minutes

Cooking Time: 30 minutes

Servings: 4

Ingredients: :

- 1 tablespoon lime juice
- 1 tablespoon olive oil,
- ½ tablespoon soy sauce
- ½ tablespoon chili powder
- ¼ tablespoon minced garlic
- 453 g boneless pork tenderloin

Directions: :

1. Set to 370 F. In a large zip-top plastic bag, mix together the lime juice, olive oil, soy sauce, chili powder, and garlic and mix well. Add the pork, seal, and refrigerate for at least 1 hour or overnight.
2. Spray a fryer basket lightly with olive oil.
3. Shake off any excess marinade from the pork and place it in the fryer basket.
4. Air fry for 15 minutes. Flip the tenderloin over and cook until the pork reaches an internal temperature of at least 145°F an additional 5 minutes. If necessary, continue to cook in 2- to 3-minute intervals until it reaches the proper temperature.
5. Let the tenderloin rest for 10 minutes before cutting into slices and serving.

Nutrition: Calories: 250, Fat: 11g, Fiber: 10.1 g, Carbs: 30.1g, Protein: 9.5g

69. Parmesan Spiced Pork Chops

Preparation Time: 10 minutes

Cooking Time: 15 minutes

Servings: 4

Ingredients: :

- 4 pork chops, boneless
- 4 tbsp parmesan cheese, grated
- 128 g pork rind
- 2 eggs, lightly beaten
- 1/2 tsp chili powder
- 1/2 tsp onion powder
- 1 tsp paprika
- 1/4 tsp pepper
- 1/2 tsp salt

Directions: :

1. Preheat the air fryer to 400 F.
2. Season pork chops with pepper and salt.
3. Add pork rind in food processor and process until crumbs form.
4. Mix together pork rind crumbs and seasoning in a large bowl.
5. Place egg in a separate bowl.
6. Dip pork chops in egg mixture then coat with pork crumb mixture and place in the air fryer basket.
7. Cook pork chops for 12-15 minutes.
8. Serve and enjoy.

Nutrition: Calories: 330, Fat: 8.9g, Fiber:12.1g, Carbs: 67g, Protein: 18.4 g

70. Creamy Pork Curry

Preparation Time: 10 minutes

Cooking Time: 37 minutes

Servings: 8

Ingredients: :

- 1kg pork shoulder, boneless and cut into chunks
- Two garlic cloves, minced
- One onion, chopped
- 384 g chicken broth
- 256 g of coconut milk
- 1/2 tsp turmeric
- 2 tbsp olive oil
- 1/2 tbsp ground cumin
- 1 1/2 tbsp curry paste
- 2 tbsp fresh ginger, grated
- 1 tablespoon Pepper
- 1 tablespoon Salt

Directions: :

1. Add oil into the pot and set the container on sauté mode.
2. Season meat with pepper and salt. Add chicken to the pot and cook until browned.
3. Add remaining Ingredients and stir everything well.
4. Seal pot with lid and cook on soup/stew mode for 30 minutes.
5. Once done, then release pressure using the quick-release method than open the lid.
6. Stir well and serve.

Nutrition: Calories 877, Fat 68.6 g, Carbohydrates 7.2 g, Sugar 2.9 g, Protein 56.5 g, Fiber: 11g

71. Texas Baby Back Ribs

Preparation Time: 20 minutes

Cooking Time: 30-40 minutes

Servings:

Ingredients: :

- 1 rack of baby back ribs,
- 2 tbsp. Oil
- 1 tbsp. Liquid Smoke
- SEASONING:
- 1 teaspoon Chili powder
- 1 teaspoon Onion powder
- 2 teaspoons Kosher Salt
- 1 teaspoon Ground Black Pepper
- ½ teaspoon Brown Sugar
- ½ teaspoon Garlic powder

Directions: :

1. Use a kitchen paper towel to pat dry the ribs, and then rub oil and liquid smoke all over it
2. All the seasonings must be mixed together in a bowl and spice the ribs with it
3. Cut the rack of ribs into 4-5 sections to fit the air fryer.
4. Depending on the rib thickens, set the air fryer to cook the ribs at 400f for 30-40 minutes and it's done

Nutrition: Calories: 187, Fat: 1.4g, Fiber: 2.1g, Carbs: 9.7g, Protein: 2.1g

72. Bratwurst Bites with Spicy Mustard

Preparation Time: 20 minutes

Cooking Time: 10 minutes

Servings: 5-6

Ingredients: :

- ⅛ Tsp. Spices, allspice, ground
- 64 g German stone ground mustard
- 6 pcs bell peppers, mini sweet peppers
- 5 links pork link sausage
- 64 g dark beer
- 3 tablespoons Honey, strained or extracted
- ½ teaspoon Spices, turmeric, ground

Directions: :

1. Mix honey, turmeric, beer and allspice in a small saucepan and boil on a low-medium heat, uncovered, until volume has reduced by half, about 8 minutes. Stir in mustard and set aside until ready to serve.
2. Place sweet peppers and bratwurst chunks in a single layer in the air fryer basket.
3. Let it cook at 400F using an air fryer for about 10 minutes, tossing once halfway through cooking, until peppers are tender and bratwurst edges are golden brown and crisp.
4. Serve warm with mustard sauce.

Nutrition: Calories: 127 Fat: 10.4g, Fiber: 3.1g Carbs: 19.7gProtein: 24.1g

73. Oriental Pork Meatballs

Preparation Time: 20 minutes

Cooking Time: 9-10 minutes

Servings: 8

Ingredients: :

- 1kg ground pork
- 2 large eggs
- 32 g chopped green onions
- 32 g chopped fresh cilantro or parsley
- 1 tablespoon minced fresh ginger
- 3 cloves garlic, minced
- 2 teaspoons soy sauce
- 1 teaspoon oyster sauce
- ½ teaspoon kosher salt
- 1 teaspoon black pepper

Directions: :

1. In the bowl, combine the pork, eggs, green onions, cilantro, ginger, garlic, soy sauce, oyster sauce, salt, and pepper. Let it mix until Ingredients are incorporated, 2 to 3 minutes. Form the mixture into 12 meatballs and arrange in a single layer in the air fryer basket.
2. Set the air fryer to 350°F for 10 minutes. U. Transfer the meatballs to a bowl and serve.

Nutrition: Calories: 117 Fat: 3.4g, Fiber: 1.1g Carbs: 9.7g, Protein: 7.1g

74.   Hungarian Beef Goulash

Preparation Time: 20 minutes

Cooking Time: 1 hr.

Servings: 6-8

Ingredients: :

- Sea salt and cracked black pepper, to taste
- 1 teaspoon Hungarian paprika
- 1 ½ kg beef chuck roast, boneless, cut into bite-sized cubes - 2 teaspoons sunflower oil
- 1 medium-sized leek, chopped
- 2 garlic cloves, minced - 2 bay leaves
- 1 teaspoon caraway seeds. - 256 g roasted vegetable broth
- 1 ripe tomato, pureed - 2 tablespoons red wine
- 2 bell peppers, chopped
- 1 celery stalk, peeled and diced

Directions: :

1. Add the salt, black pepper, Hungarian paprika, and beef to a resealable bag; shake to coat well. Heat the oil in a Dutch oven over a medium-high flame; sauté the leeks, garlic, bay leaves, and caraway seeds about 4 minutes or until fragrant. Transfer to a lightly greased baking pan. Then, brown the beef, occasionally stirring, working in batches. Add to the baking pan.

2. Add the vegetable broth, tomato, and red wine. Lower the pan onto the Air Fryer basket. Bake at 325 degrees F for 40 minutes. Add the bell peppers and celery. Cook an additional 20 minutes. Serve immediately and enjoy!

Nutrition: Calories: 306 Fat: 11g, Fiber: 8g Carbs: 37g Protein: 7.4.g

75. Coffee Rubbed Steaks

Preparation Time: 10 minutes

Cooking Time: 15 minutes

Servings: 4

Ingredients: :

- 1 and ½ tablespoons coffee, ground
- 4 rib eye steaks - ½ tablespoon sweet paprika
- 2 tablespoons chili powder
- 2 teaspoons garlic powder
- 2 teaspoons onion powder
- ¼ teaspoon ginger, ground
- ¼ teaspoon, coriander, ground
- A pinch of cayenne pepper
- Black pepper to the taste

Directions: :

1. In a bowl, mix coffee with paprika, chili powder, garlic powder, onion powder, ginger, coriander, cayenne and black pepper, stir, rub steaks with this mix, put in preheated air fryer and cook at 360 degrees F for 15 minutes.
2. Divide steaks on plates and serve with a side salad. Enjoy!

Nutrition: Calories: 296 Fat: 10.6g Fiber: 13.5g, Carbs: 50g Protein: 11g

76.   Beef Roll-ups

Preparation Time: 60 minutes

Cooking Time: 25-30 minutes

Servings: 6

Ingredients: :

- 1½ kg sirloin steak, cut into slices
- 2 tablespoons Worcestershire sauce
- ½ tablespoon garlic powder
- ½ tablespoon onion powder
- 2 medium bell peppers of any color, cut into thin strips
- 64 g shredded mozzarella cheese
- 1 tablespoon Salt
- 1 tablespoon Freshly ground black pepper
- 1 tablespoon Olive oil

Directions: :

1. Set to 370 F. Using a meat mallet, kg the steaks very thin.
2. In a small bowl, combine the Worcestershire sauce, garlic powder, and onion powder to make a marinade.
3. Place the steaks and marinade in a large zip-top plastic bag, seal, and refrigerate for at least 30 minutes. Soak 8 toothpicks in water for 15 to 20 minutes.
4. Place ¼ of the bell peppers and ¼ of the mozzarella cheese in the center of each steak. Season with salt and black pepper. Roll each steak up tightly and secure with 2 toothpicks.
5. Spray a fryer basket lightly with olive oil. Place the beef roll-ups in the fryer basket, toothpick side down, in a single layer. You may need to cook the roll-ups in batches.
6. Air fry for 10 minutes. Flip the steaks over and cook until the meat reaches an internal temperature of at least 150°F, an additional 7 to 10 minutes.
7. Let the roll-ups rest for 10 minutes before serving.

Nutrition: Calories: 287, Fat: 9.7g, Fiber: 13.71g, Carbs: 32g, Protein: 13.8g

77. Beef Chimichangas

Preparation Time: 20 minutes

Cooking Time: 25-30 minutes

Servings: 4

Ingredients: :

- 1 tablespoon Olive oil
- 453 glean ground beef
- 1 tablespoon taco seasoning
- 64 g salsa
- 1 (168 g) can fat-free refried beans
- 4 large whole-wheat tortillas
- 64 g shredded Cheddar cheese

Directions: :

1. Set to 370F. Spray fryer basket lightly with olive oil.
2. In a large skillet over medium heat, cook the ground beef until browned, about 5 minutes. Add the taco seasoning and salsa and stir to combine. Set aside.
3. Spread 64 g of refried beans onto each tortilla, leaving a ½ inch border around the edge. Add ¼ of the ground beef mixture to each tortilla and sprinkle with 2 tablespoons of Cheddar cheese.
4. Fold the opposite sides of the tortilla in and roll up.
5. Place the chimichangas in the fryer basket, seam side down. Spray lightly with olive oil. You may need to cook the chimichangas in batches.
6. Air fry until golden brown, 5 to 10 minutes.

Nutrition: Calories: 270, Fat: 54g, Fiber: 8.7gg, Carbs: 31.8g, Protein: 10.6g

78.   Mushroom and Beef Meatballs

Preparation Time: 20 minutes

Cooking Time: 30 minutes

Servings: 6

Ingredients: :

- 1 tablespoon Olive oil
- 2 kg lean ground beef
- ⅔ kg finely chopped mushrooms
- 4 tablespoons chopped parsley
- 2 eggs, beaten
- 2 teaspoons salt
- 1 teaspoon freshly ground black pepper
- 128 g whole-wheat bread crumbs

Directions: :

1. Set to 390 F. Spray a fryer basket lightly with olive oil.
2. In a large bowl, mix together the beef, mushrooms, and parsley. Add the eggs, salt, and pepper and mix gently. Add the bread crumbs and mix until the bread crumbs are no longer dry. Be careful not to overmix.
3. Using a small cookie scoop, form 24 meatballs.
4. Place the meatballs in the fryer basket in a single layer and spray lightly with olive oil.
5. Air fry until the internal temperature reaches at least 160°F, 10 to 15 minutes, shaking the basket every 5 minutes for even cooking.

Nutrition: Calories: 230, Fat: 2.6g, Fiber: 9.1g, Carbs: 22.7g, Protein: 10.1g

79. Bacon-Wrapped Filet Mignon

Preparation Time: 15 minutes

Cooking Time: 5-10 minutes

Servings: 2

Ingredients: :

- 2 filet of mignon steaks
- 2 slices of bacon
- 2 toothpicks
- 1 teaspoon of freshly cracked peppercorns we use a variety of peppercorns
- 1/2 teaspoon of kosher salt
- 1 tablespoon Avocado oil

Directions: :

1. Wrap the bacon around the mignon filet and secure it with a toothpick by pressing the toothpick through the bacon and into the filet, then to the bacon on the other end of the toothpick from the filet.
2. Season the steak with the salt and pepper or the seasonings you prefer.
3. Place the mignon filet wrapped with bacon on the air fryer rack.
4. Sprinkle a small amount of avocado oil on the steak.
5. How long to cook bacon-wrapped filet mignon Air fry the steak at 375 degrees F for about 10 minutes, and then flip as one side is nice and seared while the other is not.
6. Fry air for another 5 minutes, or until the desired doneness is reached. We are pursuing a medium.

Nutrition: Calories: 277, Fat: 10.5g, Fiber: 12.5g, Carbs: 39.5g, Protein: 15.1g

80. Winter Vegetables & Lamb Stew

Preparation Time: 35 minutes

Cooking Time: 45-50 minutes

Servings: 6

Ingredients: :

- 500g stewing lamb, cubed
- 2 cloves garlic, chopped finely
- 1 tbsp. fresh thyme, chopped finely
- 1 tablespoon freshly ground pepper and salt
- 300g butternut squash, seeded and cubed
- 150g parsnip, sliced
- 150g sweet potato, cubed
- 125g celery, sliced
- 1 medium onion, chopped coarsely
- 100ml red wine
- 125ml beef stock
- 1 tbsp. olive oil

Directions: :

1. Mix the lamb with garlic, thyme and pepper and salt to taste. Mix in the squash, parsnip, sweet potato, celery and onion.
2. Pour the red wine, beef stock and olive oil over the lamb and vegetables. Close the lid.
3. Touch the MULTI COOK menu to select STEW/CURRY program, set cooking time for 45 minutes and press START Stir once or twice. Serve with rice or couscous.

Nutrition: Calories: 398, Fat: 17.5g, Fiber: 14.8g, Carbs: 48.6g, Protein: 15.9g

81. Buttered Filet Mignon

Preparation Time: 10 minutes

Cooking Time: 14 minutes

Servings: 4

Ingredients: :

- 2 (168 g) filet mignon steaks
- 1 tablespoon butter, softened
- Salt and ground black pepper, as required

Directions: :

1. Coat each steak evenly with butter and then, season with salt and black pepper.
2. Set the temperature of air fryer to 390 degrees F. Grease an air fryer basket.
3. Arrange steaks into the prepared air fryer basket.
4. Air fry for about 14 minutes, flipping once halfway through.
5. Remove from the air fryer and transfer onto serving plates.

Serve hot.

Nutrition: Calories: 403, Carbohydrate: 0g, Protein: 48.7g, Fat: 22g, Sugar: 0g

82. Lamb Korma

Preparation Time: 35 minutes

Cooking Time: 30 minutes

Servings: 8

Ingredients: :

- 1.5kg boned lamb shoulder, chopped coarsely
- 2 medium brown onions, sliced thinly
- 5cm piece fresh ginger, grated
- 3 cloves garlic, crushed
- ⅔ cup korma paste
- 3 medium tomatoes, chopped coarsely
- 64 g chicken stock
- 300ml pouring cream
- 1 cinnamon stick
- 64 g loosely packed fresh coriander leaves
- 1 fresh long red chili, sliced thinly
- 42 g roasted flaked almonds

Directions: :

1. Combine lamb, onion, ginger, garlic, paste, tomatoes, stock, cream and cinnamon in a cooker.
2. Seal lid, cook on SLOW COOK LOW TEMP for 6 hours or touch the PRESSURE COOK menu to select MEAT/POULTRY program for 25 minutes. Press START.
3. Season to taste. Discard cinnamon stick. Serve korma sprinkled with coriander, chili and almonds.

Nutrition: Calories: 378, Fat: 9.5g, Fiber: 10.1g, Carbs: 45.6g, Protein: 10.5 g

83.   Beer-Braised Short Loin

Preparation Time: 70 minutes

Cooking Time: 40 minutes

Servings: 4

Ingredients: :

- 1 ½ kg short loin
- 2 tablespoons olive oil
- 1 bottle beer
- 2-3 cloves garlic, finely minced
- 2 Turkish bay leaves

Directions: :

1. Pat the beef dry; then, tenderize the beef with a meat mallet to soften the fibers. Place it in a large-sized mixing dish.
2. Add the remaining Ingredients; toss to coat well and let it marinate for at least 1 hour.
3. Cook about 30 minutes at 395 degrees F; after that, pause the Air Fryer. Flip the meat over and cook for another 8 minutes, or until it's done.

Nutrition: Calories: 360 Fat: 14.5g, Fiber: 11.5g, Carbs: 31.9g, Protein: 15.1g

84. Lobster Wontons

Preparation Time: 20 minutes

Cooking Time: 30 minutes

Servings: 8

Ingredients: :

- For dough:
- 1 ½-kg all-purpose flour
- ½- tsp. salt
- 5- tbsp. water
- For filling:
- 2- cups minced lobster
- 2- tbsp. oil
- 2- tsp. ginger-garlic paste
- 2- tsp. soy sauce
- 2- tsp. vinegar

Directions: :

1. Mix the dough, cover it with saran wrap and set aside.
2. Mix the filling Ingredients.
3. Fold the dough and cut it into a square.
4. Place the filling in the middle.
5. Wrap the dough to cover the filling and squeeze the edges together.
6. Preheat the Air Fryer to 200° F for 5 minutes. Place in the fry bin and cook for 20 minutes.

Nutrition: Calories: 102 Fat: 2.1g, Fiber: 1.9g Carbs: 9.9g Protein: 1.8g

85.   Buffalo Chicken Sliders

Preparation Time: 15 minutes

Cooking Time: 15-20 minutes

Servings: 6-12

Ingredients: :

- 1 kg boneless, chicken breast cut into large pieces
- 4 tbsp. butter
- 3 green onions, diced
- 64 g ranch dressing
- 12 sweet Hawaiian rolls
- 64 g chicken broth
- 3/4 l Frank's Buffalo Sauce
- 1 tbsp. dry ranch dressing mix
- 2 garlic cloves, minced
- 224 g cheddar cheese, shredded

Directions: :

1. Add chicken pieces, butter, dry ranch dressing mix, chicken broth, hot sauce, and garlic cloves to the Air fryer.
2. Pressure Cook for 15 minutes.
3. Shred chicken with forks.
4. Let the chicken soak in the prepared sauce for a couple of minutes.
5. Fill each roll with buffalo chicken, cheese, ranch, and green onions and serve.

Nutrition: Calories: 287, Fat: 10.5g, Fiber: 5.4g, Carbs: 39.5g, Protein: 10.1g

86. Beef Jerky

Preparation Time: 30 minutes

Cooking Time: 60 minutes

Servings: 4

Ingredients: :

- 128ml beer
- 64ml tamari sauce
- 1 teaspoon liquid smoke
- 2 garlic cloves, minced
- 1 teaspoon Sea salt and ground black pepper
- 1 teaspoon ancho chili powder
- 2 tablespoons honey
- 3/4-kg flank steak, slice into strips

Directions: :

6. Place all Ingredients in a ceramic dish; let it marinate for 3 hours in the refrigerator. Slice the beef into thin strips Marinate the beef in the refrigerator overnight. Now, discard the marinade and hang the meat in the cooking basket by using skewers. Air fry at 190 degrees f degrees for 1 hour. Store it in an airtight container for up to 2 weeks.

Nutrition: Calories: 155, Fat: 2.1g, Fiber: 1.9g, Carbs: 10.1g, Protein: 11.1g

87. Smoked Bacon Bread

Preparation Time: 15 minutes

Cooking Time: 30 minutes

Servings: 6

Ingredients: :

- 453 g white bread; cubed
- 453 g smoked bacon; cooked and chopped.
- 226 g cheddar cheese; shredded
- 226 g Monterey jack cheese; shredded
- 500g canned tomatoes; chopped.
- 32 g avocado oil - 1 red onion; chopped.
- 2 tbsp. chicken stock
- 2 tbsp. chives; chopped. - 8 eggs; whisked
- 2 tbsp. Salt and black pepper to taste

Directions: :

1. Add the oil to your air fryer and heat it up at 350°F
2. Add all other Ingredients except the chives and cook for 30 minutes, shaking halfway. Divide between plates and serve with chives sprinkled on top

Nutrition: Calories: 215 Fat: 3.5g, Fiber: 8.6g Carbs: 21.8g Protein: 6.4 g

88. Honey BBQ Bacon Sandwiches

Preparation Time: 10 minutes

Cooking Time: 7 minutes

Servings: 4

Ingredients: :

- 96 g BBQ sauce
- 2 tablespoons honey
- 8 bacon slices, cooked and cut into thirds
- 1 red bell pepper, sliced
- 1 yellow bell pepper, sliced
- 3 pita pockets, halved
- 1 and 32 g butter lettuce leaves, torn
- 2 tomatoes, sliced

Directions: :

1. In a bowl, mix BBQ sauce with honey and whisk well.
2. Brush bacon and all bell peppers with some of this mix, place them in your air fryer and cook at 350 degrees F for 4 minutes.
3. Shake fryer and cook them for 2 minutes more.
4. Stuff pita pockets with bacon mix, also stuff with tomatoes and lettuce, spread the rest of the BBQ sauce.

Nutrition: Calories: 415, Fat: 19.4g, Fiber: 12.5g, Carbs: 37.5g, Protein: 29.5g

89. Pizza Hot Dog Buns

Preparation Time: 15 minutes

Cooking Time: 10 minutes

Servings: 2

Ingredients: :

- Hot dogs (2)
- Pepperoni (4 slices - halved)
- Pizza sauce (300g)
- Hot dog buns (2)
- Mozzarella cheese (300g)
- Sliced olives (2 tsp.)

Directions: :

1. Warm the Air Fryer at 390° Fahrenheit.
2. Make four slits down each hot dog and place them in the Air Fryer basket. Set the timer for 3 minutes. Transfer to a cutting board.
3. Place a pepperoni half in each slit of the hot dogs. Portion the pizza sauce between buns and fill with the hot dogs, mozzarella cheese, and olives.
4. Return the hot dogs back into the fryer basket and cook until buns are crisp and cheese is melted (2 min.).

Nutrition: Calories: 221, Fat: 4.7g, Fiber: 5.2g, Carbs: 45.8g, Protein: 10.5 g

90. Philly Chicken Stromboli

Preparation Time: 30 minutes

Cooking Time: 15-20 minutes

Servings: 4

Ingredients: :

- Vegetable oil (1 tsp.)
- Onion (half of 1)
- Chicken breasts (2/total of 453 g)
- Worcestershire sauce (1 tbsp.)
- Pizza dough (14 oz. pkg. - homemade or store-bought)
- Freshly cracked black pepper & salt
- Cheese Whiz or your favorite cheese sauce (200g)
- Grated Cheddar cheese (100g)

Directions: :

1. Warm the Cheese Whiz in the microwave.
2. Set the temperature to 400° Fahrenheit in the Air Fryer.
3. Place the onion in the fryer for eight minutes – shaking gently halfway through the cycle. Thinly slice and add the chicken and Worcestershire sauce, salt, and pepper – tossing evenly. Air fry for another eight minutes – stirring several times. Remove and let the mixture cool.
4. Lightly flour a flat surface and press out the dough into a rectangle of 11x13 (the long side facing you). Sprinkle half of the cheddar over the dough. Leave a one-inch border - topping it off with the onion/chicken mixture.
5. Drizzle the warmed cheese sauce over the top, finishing with the rest of the cheddar cheese.
6. Roll the Stromboli toward the empty corner (away from you). Keep the filling tight and tuck in the ends. Arrange it seam side down and shape in a "U" to fit into the basket. Slice four slits in the top with the tip of a knife.
7. Lightly brush the top with a little oil. Set the temperature to 370° Fahrenheit.
8. Spray the basket and add the Stromboli. Fry for 12 minutes – turning about halfway through the cooking process.
9. Use a serving platter and invert the tasty treat from the basket. Arrange it on a cutting board and cut into three-inch segments. Serve with ketchup for dipping.

Nutrition: Calories: 315 Fat: 8.5g, Fiber: 7.5g Carbs: 45.9g, Protein: 18.5 g

91.   Chicken and Avocado Sliders

Preparation Time: 30 minutes

Cooking Time: 10-15 minutes

Servings: 4

Ingredients: :

- 300g ground chicken meat
- 4 burger buns
- 64 g Romaine lettuce, loosely packed
- ½ teaspoon dried parsley flakes
- 1/3 teaspoon mustard seeds
- 1 teaspoon onion powder
- 1 ripe fresh avocado, mashed
- 1 teaspoon garlic powder
- 1 ½ tablespoon extra-virgin olive oil
- 1 cloves garlic, minced
- 1 teaspoon Nonstick cooking spray
- 1 teaspoon Salt and cracked black pepper (peppercorns), to taste

Directions: :

1. Firstly, spritz an air fryer cooking basket with a nonstick cooking spray.
2. Mix ground chicken meat, mustard seeds, garlic powder, onion powder, parsley, salt, and black pepper until everything is thoroughly combined. Make sure not to overwork the meat to avoid tough chicken burgers.
3. Shape the meat mixture into patties and roll them in breadcrumbs; transfer your burgers to the prepared cooking basket. Brush the patties with the cooking spray.
4. Air-fry at 355 F for 9 minutes, working in batches. Slice burger buns into halves. In the meantime, combine olive oil with mashed avocado and pressed garlic.
5. To finish, lay Romaine lettuce and avocado spread on bun bottoms; now, add burgers and bun tops. Bon appétit!

Nutrition: Calories: 328 Fat: 7.5g, Fiber: 9.1g Carbs: 48.7g Protein: 18.1g

92.   Cornbread with Pulled Pork

Preparation Time: 30 minutes

Cooking Time: 20 minutes

Servings: 6

Ingredients: :

- 1kg pulled pork, leftover works well too
- 1 teaspoon dried rosemary - 1/2 teaspoon chili powder
- 3 cloves garlic, peeled and pressed
- 1/2 recipe cornbread in box
- 1/2 tablespoon brown sugar
- 96 g scallions, thinly sliced - 1 teaspoon sea salt

Directions: :

1. Preheat a large-sized nonstick skillet over medium heat; now, cook the scallions together with the garlic and pulled pork. Next, add the sugar, chili powder, rosemary, and salt. Cook, stirring occasionally, until the mixture is thickened. Preheat your air fryer to 335 degrees F. Now, coat two mini loaf pans with a cooking spray. Add the pulled pork mixture and spread over the bottom using a spatula. Spread the previously prepared cornbread batter over top of the spiced pulled pork mixture.

2. Bake this cornbread in the preheated air fryer until a tester inserted into the center of it comes out clean, or for 18 minutes. Bon appétit!

Nutrition: Calories: 386 Fat: 11.8g, Fiber: 9.4gg Carbs: 34.9g Protein: 10.5g

93. Chicken Skin Crisps

Preparation Time: 20 minutes

Cooking Time: 15 minutes

Servings: 4

Ingredients: :

- 453 g Chicken Skin
- ½ Teaspoon Black Pepper
- 1 Teaspoon Dill
- ½ Teaspoon Chili Flakes
- 1 Teaspoon Butter
- ½ Teaspoon Sea Salt, Fine

Directions: :

1. Slice your chicken skin roughly, and then sprinkle it with your seasoning.
2. Mix you're the chicken skin, and melt your butter before adding it.
3. Preheat your air fryer to 360, and then place your chicken skin in your air fryer basket.
4. Cook for three minutes per side, and then serve warm or room temperature.

Nutrition: Calories: 166, Fat: 87g, Fiber: 3.1g, Carbs: 4.7g, Protein: 12.1g

94.   Beef Empanadas

Preparation Time: 10 minutes

Cooking Time: 20 minutes

Servings: 4

Ingredients: :

- 1 tsp. water
- 1 egg white
- 1 C. picadillo
- 8 Goya empanada discs (thawed)

Directions: :

Ensure your Air Fryer is preheated to 325. Spray basket with olive oil.

Place 2 tablespoons of picadillo into the center of each disc. Fold disc in half and use a fork to seal edges. Repeat with all Ingredients.

Whisk egg white with water and brush tops of empanadas with egg wash.

Add 2-3 empanadas to the Air Fryer.

Close air fryer lid. Set temperature to 325°F, and set time to 8 minutes, cook until golden. Repeat till you cook all filled empanadas.

Nutrition: Calories: 195, Fat: 3.4g, Fiber: 8.1g, Carbs: 19.7g, Protein: 12.2 g

95.   Air Fryer Duck Breast

Preparation Time: 5 Minutes

Cooking Time: 15 Minutes

Servings: 2

Ingredients:

- Duck breast: Choose boneless duck breast. You can use wild duck or farmed duck. Note that the farmed type often gives a fattier duck breast.
- Salt and pepper: This recipe uses salt and pepper for a simple seasoning, but you can add other flavors if you like. Some great options are:
- Chinese five-spice
- Allspice
- Rosemary and thyme
- Add around ¼ teaspoon per duck breast of any additional seasoning.

Directions:

1. Step 1: Prepare the duck breast. Pat the duck breast dry with a paper towel. Then score the duck skin through into the fat. A crosshatch pattern is traditional, or you can use parallel lines which is what you often see in restaurants.
2. This step is needed to allow the fat to render easily, and to help the skin to get really crispy. You should avoid cutting all the way through into the meat as this can add more moisture to the skin during cooking, preventing it from getting crispy.
3. Step 2: Season duck breast. Season with salt and pepper. Add any other seasoning that you want in the same way.
4. Step 3: Air fry duck breast. Place duck breast in the air fryer basket skin-side up, and air fry at 390°F/ 195°C for 5 minutes. When the time is up, turn the temperature down to 320°F/ 160°C, and air fry duck breast for an additional 10-12 minutes.

5. Starting the cooking at a higher temperature, before reducing the temperature, allows the fat to render more quickly, so that the skin should get crispy before the meat becomes overcooked.

6. If your air fryer starts smoking during cooking, stop your air fryer, drain the fat out, and resume cooking. You may need to do this more than once depending on how fatty your duck breast is. Note: farmed duck tends to be fattier than wild duck.

7. When the cooking time is finished, check the internal temperature with an instant read meat thermometer. USDA recommends cooking duck breasts to an internal temperature of 165°F/ 74°C, which will be well done. Some people prefer medium-rare (130°F/ 54°C), medium (140°F/ 60°C), or medium-well done 155°F (68°F).

8. Step 4: Rest duck breasts. Remove from the air fryer to a plate and cover with aluminum foil for 5-10 minutes.

Nutrition:

CALORIES: 485TOTAL FAT: 26gsaturated FAT: 7gtrans FAT: 0gunsaturated FAT: 17gcholesterol: 326mgsodium: 516mgcarbohydrates: 0gfiber: 0gsugar: 0gprotein: 59g

96. Rib-Eye Steaks

Preparation Time: 5 mins

Cooking Time: 15 mins

Servings: 2

Ingredients:

- 2 rib-eye steaks, cut 1 1/2- inch thick
- ½ cup reduced-sodium soy sauce
- ¼ cup olive oil
- 4 teaspoons grill seasoning (such as Montreal Steak Seasoning®)

Direction:

1. Combine steaks, soy sauce, olive oil, and seasoning in a large resealable bag. Marinate meat for at least 2 hours.
2. Remove steaks from the bag and discard marinade. Pat excess oil off steaks.
3. Add about 1 tablespoon water to the bottom of the air fryer pan to prevent it from smoking during cooking. Preheat the air fryer to 400 degrees F (200 degrees C).
4. Cook steaks in the preheated air fryer for 7 minutes, flip, and cook about 7 minutes more for medium-rare. For a medium, cook 8 minutes per side.
5. Let steaks sit for about 5 minutes before serving.

Nutrition: Calories: 652, Fat: 49g, Carbs: 8g, Protein: 44g

97. Air Fryer Fried Chicken

Preparation Time: 15 mins

Cooking Time: 45 mins

Servings: 4 to 6

Ingredients: :

For the chicken:

- 1 4-pound fryer chicken, cut into 10 pieces (2 breasts cut in half, 2 wings, 2 legs, 2 thighs)
- 1 teaspoon kosher salt
- 1 teaspoon ground black pepper
- 2 cups buttermilk

For the coating:

- 2 cups all-purpose flour
- 1 tablespoon season salt (such as Lawry's)
- 1 teaspoon kosher salt
- 1 teaspoon ground black pepper
- 1 tablespoon garlic powder
- 1 tablespoon paprika
- Spray olive oil for cooking

Directions: :

Marinate the chicken:

1. Season the chicken well with salt and pepper and then add it to a bowl with buttermilk. Chicken pieces should be covered with the buttermilk.
2. Let it sit for at least an hour or up to overnight.

Bread the chicken:

3. To prepare the breading mixture, stir together flour, seasoned salt, salt, pepper, garlic powder, and paprika.

4. Remove chicken pieces from buttermilk and shake off any excess; then dip in the flour mix and coat well. Transfer breaded

5. chicken pieces to a clean plate or wire rack to rest.

Air-fry the chicken:

6. You will need to work in two batches if you are doing a full chicken. Spray the basket of your air fryer with nonstick spray. Place half of the pieces in the basket of your air fryer. Try to ensure the pieces don't touch. Air needs to circulate around them.

7. Spray the chicken pieces lightly with spray oil. Place the basket in the air fryer and turn the air fryer to 350°F. Cook for 14 minutes, then flip the fried chicken with tongs, spray lightly with oil a second time on the bottom side of the chicken, and cook for another 10 to 12 minutes, until white meat reaches 165°F and dark meat reaches 175°F (I find that cooking the dark meat a little more makes it more tender).

8. During the air frying process, if you pull out the chicken and notice any dry flour spots on the chicken, spray those spots lightly with oil. The breading will never crisp up if it doesn't have a tiny bit of oil to hydrate it. It will just burn.

Serve:

9. When the fried chicken is ready, let it rest on a plate for a few minutes before serving. Serve immediately with salad, coleslaw, mashed potatoes, or your favorite fried chicken sides!

10. Cooked fried chicken can be stored in the fridge for 5 days and reheated in a 300°F oven for 8 to 10 minutes.

Nutrition: Calories 389, Fat 17g, Carbs 22g, Protein 36g

98. Air Fryer Meat Balls

Preparation Time: **10** mins

Cooking Time: 10 mins

Servings: 4

Ingredients:

- 1 pound ground beef
- 1 small onion minced (about ¼ cup)
- ½ teaspoon salt
- ½ teaspoon pepper
- ½ teaspoon dry mustard

Direction:

1. In a medium Bowl, combine the ground beef with the onion, salt, pepper, and dry mustard.
2. Scoop the meat into 2-3 inches meatballs.
3. Lightly brust the air fryer basket with olive oil, or line with parchment paper.
4. Cook at 380 degree Fahrenheit for 7-10 minutes.
5. Serve warm.

Nutrition: Calories: 297, Fat: 23g, Carbs: 2g, Protein: 20g

99.   Air Fryer Top Round Roast

Preparation Time: 5 mins

Cooking Time: **48** mins

Servings: 4

Ingredients:

- 3 pound beef top round roast
- ½ teaspoon salt
- ¼ teaspoon pepper
- ¼ cup beef broth
- 16 ounces mini potatoes
- 16 ounces baby carrots

Direction:

1. Prepare the roast, by slightly coating it with onlive oile, and sprinkling the salt and pepper to coat both sides.
2. Preheat the oven to 400 degree Fahrenheit.
3. Place the roat in the basket, and cook at 400 degrees. Cook for 25-28 minutes.
4. While the roast is cooking, toss the carrots and potatoes in olive oil, salt and pepper. Let sit until the top of the roast is done cooking.
5. Once the roast has cooked the first 25-28 minutes, turn the roast over, baste with beef broth and add the prepared carrots and potatoes. Return the basket to the the the air fryer and cook at 400 deree for an additional 18-20 minutes.
6. Potatoes and carrots should be soft , and the internal temperature of the roast is 145 degrees. Allow the rost to rest for 5-10 minutes before servng.

Nutrition: Calories: 214, Fat: 49g, Carbs: 121g, Protein: 308g

100. Air Fryer Beef Roast

Preparation Time: 15 minutes

Cooking Time: 1 hour

Servings: 6

Ingredients:

- 3 Lb beef chuck roast
- 1 tsp skeak seasoning
- 1 Package Gluten-Free or Regular Brown Gravy Mix.
- ½ cup water
- 4 tsps Unsalted Butter
- Parsley or Rosemary to Garnish

Direction:

1. Begin by preheating the air fryer to 390 degree F for about 5 minutes.
2. While this is preheating, season the roast evenly with steak seasoning.
3. Combine the Gravy with ½ cup water and set aside.
4. Once the preheating time is up, carefully spray the air fryer with cooking oil of choice such as grapeseed oil.
5. Place the roast in the air fryer and let it cook at 390*F for 15 minutes. This will sear the outside.
6. Once cooking time is up, prepare s sheet of foil to place the roast on.
7. Carefully remove the roast from air fryer and place it on foil.
8. Roll the foil up around the roast and place it back in the air fryer.
9. At this point be sure the foil is up around the sides of the roast to be sur that air will still circulate.
10. Carefully pour the Brown Gravy mixture over the roast, evenly.
11. Place the butter on the top of the roast.
12. Cook at 340*F for 30-40 minutes until the internal temperature reach atleast 145*F.
13. Once done, let rest for 5 minutes, slice and serve.
14. Roast can be served with dippings as a gravy.

Nutrition: Calories: 620, Fat: 43g, Carbs: 3g, Protein: 56g

101. Air Fryer Steak Wrapped Asparagus

Preparation Time: 10 mins

Cooking Time: 10 mins

Servings: 6

Ingredients:

- 1 pound Aparagus (Trimmed)
- 2 cups grape Tomatoeas (Halved)
- 4 Tsps Balsamic Vinegar
- 1 ½ pound Skirt Steak or Flank Steak (Thiny Sliced)
- 4 Tsps Olive Oil
- 1 Clove Garlic (Crushed)
- 1 Tsp salt
- Olive Oil Coking Spray

Direction:

1. Spray the basket of the Ninja Foodi lightly with oliveoil spray.
2. Slice the steak against the grain into 6 pieces, as evenly as possible.
3. In a small bowl, combine the vinegar, oil, garlic, and salt. Just slightly mix it.It's not going to fully combined.
4. Take about 3 asparagus and place thm in one slice of steak, roll it up and place it in the basket of the Ninja Foodi.
5. Continue this process for all of the steak. For this recipe, the basket will fit 3 at a time.
6. Once there are 3 in the basket, add in half of the tomatoes.
7. Using a Brush, brush the steak and vegetables with olive oil and vinegar mixture.
8. Cooking Using the air crisp function at 390 degree for 10 minutes using the attached lid with the Ninja Foodi. (Note-I do recommend checking on them at 5 minutes. We prefer them cook until 10 minutes but your desires doneness may vary).
9. Carefully remove and repeat the process for the remaining 3 steakes.
10. Serve the steak wrapped asparagus with tomaotes.

Nutrition: Calories: 432, Fat: 29g, Carbs: 7g, Protein: 34g

CONCLUSION

An air fryer is an excellent electronic appliance that allows you to cook food at lower temperatures than conventional ovens. It is a fast and easy way to cook, low on fat and calories.

When you need a delicious and healthy meal, it is always good to know what you are eating. Air fryer toaster oven can help you do that.

You can maintain a healthy eating habit by air frying foods because it provides you with the perfect amount of flavor, texture, and color. You will not have to worry about your food's nutrition because this appliance only cooks food with the minimum amount of Ingredients possible.

You can also use the air fryer to make grilled foods that are baked in a low heat environment, making them very moist, crispy on the outside. You can also use Air Fryer to make fish and poultry products that are soft and lip-smacking. Air Fryer oven is a kitchen appliance used to heat up and cook food quickly. This device comes with many benefits like it is easy to clean up, fast, perfect for making a meal for one person, less fuel consumption, less noise level, small size, and many more benefits. Air fryers cook food from all angles, so all the food surfaces get cooked at the same time. This helps lock in moisture, so your food has less chance of drying out or losing its taste and color. You'll find that most of the time, you don't even need to flip your food while air frying!

Air fryers are great, mostly when you use them for cooking fabulous meals like meatballs, chicken, fish, or vegetables.

Air frying also results in a crispy surface free of oil because it doesn't need to be heated as it cooks through the food. Because it's also cooked through, your food will be ready much faster than with other methods. It's even more convenient and easy to clean up after cooking with an air fryer than with other methods. Compared with conventional baking and roasting methods, air frying results in a leaner fat-free menu, a leaner calorie-filled meal, and an overall healthier diet!

When you use your air fryer, all of your food is cooked in oven-like temperatures, so you can use any recipes that work in an ordinary oven. The health benefits of an air fryer are undeniable. Not only does it promote weight loss and fends off obesity, but it also encourages healthy living and good nutrition. An air fryer does not make food unhealthy when it cooks it – all you need to do is make sure you use quality Ingredients to prepare your meals. The air fryer is ideal for making snacks for the whole family when everyone wants different food types.

So, there's no reason not to own an air fryer.

I hope you have learned something!

Printed in Great Britain
by Amazon

24360906R00064